A Century of Twickenham Legends

David Llewellyn

Articles by Dai Llewellyn
Images © Getty Images;

Matador
9 Priory Business Park
Kibworth Beauchamp
Leicestershire LE8 0RX, UK
Tel: (+44) 116 279 2299
Fax: (+44) 116 279 2277
Email: books@troubador.co.uk
Web: www.troubador.co.uk/matador

ISBN 978 1848765 634

British Library Cataloguing in Publication Data.
A catalogue record for this book is available from the British Library.

Typeset in 12pt Garamond by Troubador Publishing Ltd, Leicester, UK

Matador is an imprint of Troubador Publishing Ltd

To the memory of Billy Williams who had the foresight to purchase an old cabbage patch in Twickenham just over a hundred years ago, the produce of which has subsequently given pleasure to millions.

Introduction, Part One ...

From memory it was Robin Wade, the eminent museum designer and distinguished expatriate Aussie, who first suggested the word 'wall'. It was just prior to the 1999 Rugby World Cup and the museum committee was tossing around the idea of creating some sort of Hall of Fame at the Museum of Rugby, Twickenham – as the World Rugby Museum was then known. From a little abstract rhyming (hall/wall) an entire concept, and now a book, was born....

Halls of Fame are fine in principle, whether they are hosted within a physical 'hall' or whether they remain as purely conceptual entities. For an associated museum, regular hall of fame inductions mean regular publicity and the alluring opportunity to create a stable of high profile ambassadors. In addition it is an attractive proposition to be able to recognise sporting achievement that might otherwise slowly slip from the popular memory or to 'rescue' those moments that have already fallen from view.

However, the 'hall' concept didn't sit quite so comfortably with the team at the World Rugby Museum. Halls of Fame tend to be created with the intention of existing in perpetuity and this brings a whole raft of problems. Inevitably, each new set of inductees gradually dilutes the impact of those selected before. How does it feel to be told that you're the six hundred and twenty-seventh greatest player in your particular club or sport? Can that individual really be seen in the same light as the person selected third – despite endless propaganda claiming/demanding that all inductees are viewed equally? In addition, most halls eventually succumb to the temptation to start creating hierarchies within their inductees, in an attempt to revisit those higher profile inductees who generate the most interest. Inductees are 'elevated' to Legend status, or similar, as the concept of equality is cast aside to prevent public or press interest from waning.

Rugby players would have to be very carefully selected if they were to be plucked out from the crowd in the ultimate team game and how would the hall sit within a museum that placed great value on its examination of the social and political history of the sport and did not simply focus on the on-field activities? How could we maintain the museum's broad, international focus if we only selected former England players? Where in the museum would/could a hall be placed without incurring extraordinary costs for major structural work? A great deal of thinking and planning was needed and it was Robin's hall/wall rhyme that provided the answer. We were sitting within it... Twickenham Stadium.

Events from the great international rugby matches played at Twickenham would be the focus of the hall and it would not be a hall, but a wall. We would use the walls of the stadium, giving the inductees a presence within the fabric of the ground itself – the very place where the selected players had performed the feats for which they would be recognised. It seemed perfectly suited to our desires and it also ticked myriad other requirements that placated our initial concerns. England was, obviously, the home side in most international matches played at the ground but they – by virtue of practical necessity – always had an opposition on every match day, so we would select players from the ranks of the opposition teams as well, ensuring that we maintained our international remit. Better still the grand old Stadium's centenary season was only a decade away. Could we select one hundred players over the next ten years, so that the 100th inductee could be announced – and the wall completed – on the precise day that the centenary was celebrated in 2010? The opportunity was just too good to ignore – 100 great players for 100 memorable years and a finite number of individuals who would forever be inextricably linked to the ground and its first century.

Everything looked good in theory, but many details required resolution. How would we decide how the 100 slots would be allocated amongst the various nations who had taken the field at Twickenham? What would the induction criteria be? How would the inductions be announced? How exactly would the individuals be recognised around the ground? Would the wall be referenced within the Museum?

Some rather convoluted equations were needed to answer the first question and my calculator went into overdrive, estimating the likely fixtures to be held at Twickenham over the forthcoming decade, and at that point not yet knowing whether the 2007 RWC would be held in England or France. The number of appearances made by a team during the century, as a proportion of all matches played, provided them with a number of bricks in the wall. It seemed the fairest policy and, with a little tinkering as fixture lists were subsequently announced, it served the project well. England ended up with an allocation of forty-one of the one hundred bricks – having appeared in most, but not all, of the Twickenham test matches over the century. Their statistically accurate allocation would have been forty-nine, but with some of the smaller nations sitting on small portions of a single brick it was decided to reduce England's allocation to allow the other nations to receive whole bricks. Wales came next with nine bricks whilst South Africa's international isolation reduced their brick allocation slightly in comparison to the other Tri-Nations sides.

Selection criteria had to be strict to ensure that we were true to our mission. That each inductee should have played in an international fixture at Twickenham and have retired from international competition was fairly logical. However, it immediately removed from contention a raft of pre-eminent Southern Hemisphere players, such as Danie Craven, who never featured in a test match at Twickenham, because they played in an era when tours of the United Kingdom could be a decade apart rather than an annual contractual obligation. The requirement that a player be retired proved incredibly problematic when it came to Jonny Wilkinson. Jonny was, quite clearly, entirely worthy of contention due to countless superb performances at Twickenham over the last decade of the Stadium's first century. However, despite the very best efforts of his body to let him down at every turn, he did not retire while the wall was being constructed and so was never eligible for inclusion. Fittingly, Johnny kicked off the 2010 game against Wales when the centenary was celebrated and the wall was concluded. I would suggest that Jonny might be the sole individual for whom the rules could be bent, due to his enormous impact at Twickenham, and who could be considered for inclusion as a special 101st inductee when he finally hangs up his boots.

The final two prerequisites of induction were used in concert and allowed us to avoid the selection of 100 players who were all try-scoring, match winning wingers. A player was to have achieved 'greatness' in their career but must also have added something to the 'magic' of Twickenham. Players like Martin Johnson, Brian Moore and Jason Leonard put in a series of incredible performances at the ground and, despite never having run the entire length of the field at the last minute to score in the corner, they undoubtedly added something to the mythology and sense of the place. However, a player like Obolensky, Wilson-Shaw or Oti could still qualify on the basis of a sublime moment or a single game where they achieved greatness – even if only fleetingly – if they added something to the ground's collective memory. The design of the 'bricks' themselves was another cute concept. Blue plaques, aping the round heritage plaques found on historic houses, would be created to acknowledge each inductee, but shaped as a rugby ball oval.

The selection process was a complicated, prolonged and completely satisfying experience that took many shapes and involved many individuals. Members of the public offered up names (and rationale) for inclusion and the Museum's staff and committee thrashed out names in long discussions. Special mention should be made to another member of the museum committee, Richard Steele, whose encyclopaedic knowledge of the game and its illustrious combatants allowed us to make some very difficult decisions. I still can not imagine a more enjoyable 'job' than the numerous evening sessions that we spent over a period of years sitting in Richmond pubs discussing the merits of great players over a pint.

The first inductions were made in November 2000, on the occasion of that season's England v Australia match. As was to become the standard format for many subsequent inductions two individuals were indicted together, selected from the opposing sides, and on this first occasion it was Bernard Gadney and Nick Farr-Jones. On every occasion it was my role and great pleasure to contact the former great that we inducted, to inform them of their selection and to set them up for an interview with Dai Llewellyn that would be printed in the relevant match day programme or placed on the Museum's website. These excellently crafted and insightful articles would delve into the player's feelings towards, and memories of, Twickenham Stadium and you are holding them all in your hands right now, in many places expanded to include material that had to be removed due to word count constraints.

Without exception, every inductee was humbled and honoured to be recognised and I had the great privilege to speak with many of the greatest players of the 20th century. Particular highlights included picking up the receiver in the middle of the night to dial Colin Meads at his home in New Zealand and also chatting with my favourite childhood player, Andy Irvine. I was thrilled to be able to tell the wonderful Bernard Gadney of his induction, but we were shocked and saddened a matter of days later to hear that he had passed away. Sadly, his great friend and former teammate Hal Sever also passed away around the time of his own induction.

Halfway through the process, in 2005, enough names had been compiled to justify the creation of an interactive wall in the Museum's entrance area providing footage, images and statistics to help interpret the inductees and to assist those who visited on an non-event day and were therefore unable to traverse the ground viewing the plaques. Someone else who deserves mention at this point is Andrew Davie who worked so hard for us to put together the multimedia components of the Wall of Fame.

The media gathered to see a former England player unveil his plaque and the Museum's interactive wall and that player had an uncanny connection with the Wall – Martin Johnson. The future World Cup winner was captain of England on the day that the first inductions were made in 2000 and a decade later, on the day that the Wall was completed he was at Twickenham again – this time as England manager. The selection of the World Cup winning captain to open the wall in 2005 was entirely logical but was also nicely prescient. As the induction process came to a close in 2009 it was Johnson who was nominated by the public as the greatest of all the Twickenham Wall of Fame inductees. It is a title that very few could deny the man who captained his country to victory on 19 of 20 occasions at Twickenham – exactly the calibre of player and sort of achievement that the Twickenham Wall of Fame was created to honour.

Jed Smith
Melbourne, Australia Former Curator of the World Rugby Museum
May 2010

Introduction, Part Two

My first reaction when I was asked to take over the Wall of Fame was exactly the same as all of our visitors when viewing it in our galleries '…where the hell is Jason Robinson?' I thought.

The name 'Jason Robinson' being interchangeable with an overseas touring squad of other names from different eras, and different corners of the globe. Players whose names may not have been on the Wall at the time, or (whisper it) may not have made it on to Wall at all!

This reaction continues as an almost daily occurrence. A curious Welshman approaches the wall, nods respectfully at JPR, hums in reverence of Edwards before casting about for Morgan…Morgan…MORGAN…. "Where the hell is Cliff Morgan?" he shouts before cursing the English, spitting on the floor, and hastening out of the building.

It all started with Cliff Morgan really. Everybody knew the deal. There would be 100 great players carefully selected from the annals of Twickenham folklore to fairly represent 100 years of first-class international rugby. Out of respect for the many visiting sides and players that have enriched encounters at the Stadium over the years, around half of the inductees would be non-English.

As long as there were still a few slots left people seemed happy. Regular visitors would quietly peruse the Wall, rub their chin, and make a mental note to keep an eye out for the favourite player. But as the slots continued to fill and the space grew less, a quiet mania ensued. After a time visitors took to knocking on the office door, seeking reassurance about who would, and who would not, be included. The most harrowing scenes were those, children and pensioners alike, who would hover for hours in a state of tortured confusion, '…but where's Jonny?' they would say.

As the Stadium entered its 100th season and the Wall neared its completion the clamour for Cliff intensified. Visitors would recite the criteria upon which the inductees were selected, quoting the meagre as yet unfilled allocation set aside for the Welsh, and incanting dates as though possessing of some profound singular significance '….19th January 1952…18th January 1958…' and so it went on.

And when the magic number was finally reached and the 100 inductees had taken their place on the wall, with Cliff Morgan in his rightful place, that's when it really hit the fans.

Behind the scenes several emergency meetings had taken place about Jonny Wilkinson. His contributions were as great, if not greater than any other individual during Twickenham's first century, but his frankly stubborn refusal to retire rendered him ineligible for inclusion. Could we break the rules for him? Would his omission compromise the Wall's validity? Might we extend the Wall to include 101 inductees on account of there being 101 years from 1910 to 2010?

But believe it or not the final act would prove to be the most controversial. The 2010 Player of the Twickenham Century poll (Martin Johnson was voted Number One) would draw on the Wall's inductees as a long list from which rugby enthusiasts around the world could cast their vote for Twickenham's greatest ever performer. Immediately the Welsh were back in, multiple voting their men into nine of the top ten positions. Steps were taken to limit each participant to a single vote. But this on-line presence suddenly alerted the Southern hemisphere to what they immediately seized upon as evidence of an Anglo-conspiracy to debase history and undermine their sporting heritage. "Where the hell is Brian Lochore...Joost Van Der Westhuizen...Danie Gerber...John Eales...?" The angry emails swooped in from South of the Equator like enemy bombers in the night.

I replied to each and every one. Thanking them for their interest, and doing my best to flatter their countries' rich contribution to rugby, while explaining as patiently as I could that they may only have been involved in only a few games at Twickenham and as such could only receive a few spaces on the Wall.

Yet in retrospect all of this just goes to show why the Wall of Fame was such a necessary and worthy project. Rugby invokes people's passions, and a fierce national pride, in a way that perhaps no other medium can. And those great competitors at the centre of the Twickenham storm, be they heroes or villains, command the rapt attention of fans and supporters around the globe in a way that no others will.

Phil McGowan
Twickenham Interpretation Officer, World Rugby Museum
May 2010

Foreword

A Wall of Fame? On the face of it, a mere wall barely does justice to its subject, unless we're talking about something akin to the Great Wall of China . What about a Hall of Fame? Or better still, a Mansion of Glory ? That sounds about right for the Serge Blancos and Hugo Portas, the Sean Fitzpatricks and Hennie Mullers...wondrous sportsmen who not only grew to their fullest size but also made it possible for the union game to broaden and ripen, to realise the best of itself. There again, it does not require much of an imaginative leap to put "wall" and "hall" together and come up with "Wallhalla", a place fit for rugby's heroes. Let's settle on "Wallhalla" and move on.

Among the many pleasures of contributing a foreword to this most handsome of additions to rugby's library is its jogging of the memory - the "winged host that soars", as Evelyn Waugh poetically put it. He wasn't thinking of rugby when he wrote those words: it is, to be sure, difficult to imagine the embittered and irritable old aesthete taking much pleasure in a double-dummy scissors or a pushover try. But memory is as much a part of sport as it is of art, and anyway, there are enough wings who soared in the list of inductees to excuse the borrowing of the phrase.

Take Philippe Saint-André as an example. When rugby followers below pensionable age talk of the greatest wings they ever saw play at international level, two names crop up time and again: David Campese, the fleet-footed, tap-dancing, hitch-kicking Wallaby who could bamboozle opponents with a single shimmy of the hips while talking the hind legs off an entire derby-full of donkeys; and Jonah Lomu, who took a slightly more direct approach to his trade while not saying anything much to anyone. Yet it was Saint-André, not obviously blessed with Campese's athletic gifts and about half the size of Lomu, who completed the "try from nowhere" at Twickenham in 1991 and created the "try from the ends of the earth" in Auckland three years later: two of the most extraordinary, least comprehensible scores in the whole history of the game.

I witnessed the first of them with my own eyes, having blagged my way into Twickenham on Grand Slam day by showing an empty seed packet - a variety of garden pea, if memory serves - to a visually-challenged gatekeeper momentarily distracted by his sudden yearning for a bacon sandwich. (Free entry for the impoverished masses was easier in those days, for there were terraces on which to stand, and to hide.) Finding myself directly beneath the Royal Box, I watched that great French try unfold from right to left. Every last act of it was perfect in conception and execution: Pierre Berbizier's impudent flick to the peerless Blanco, who was standing deep in his own in-goal area; Blanco's devil-may-care run towards danger: Philippe

Sella's precisely angled supporting run, which hinted at the presence of a slide rule embedded in his cerebral cortex; Didier Camberabero's chip-and-gather, followed by a kick across field that could not have been bettered by the celestial Zidane himself; and Saint-André's finish, which proved beyond all reasonable doubt that he was equipped with the heightened instincts of a small forest animal.

Discuss the try with him now and he will offer a few random thoughts before changing the subject to something he considers more interesting: that is to say, the front row of the scrum. Saint-André may have won dozens of caps, captained his country and forged himself a reputation as one of modern-day rugby's true attacking spirits, but in reality he was a prop in wing's clothing. During his days coaching Sale , he was heard to say the following: "People speak of the grand tradition of the French game, by which they mean the running and passing, the creativity. But the reality is that when I played, I sometimes waited an hour to see the ball Why? Because in rugby, you need people to do the bad things before others can do the nice things. Without props, there are no wings. This is why I like props more than anyone."

For a man who dealt so much in the currency of the barely believable, Saint-André had – and has – a firm grip on rugby reality. Yet when it comes to the glittering prizes, props are rarely to be found at the head of the queue. There are only five examples of the species in this current Twickenham list of the high and mighty, all of them English: Fran Cotton and Jason Leonard, substantial citizens both and well known to anyone who has lived and loved the sport for longer than five minutes; Eric Evans, Ron Jacobs and Norman Wodehouse, whose names are slowly disappearing into the mists. Measure that against the umpteen Smart-Alec outside-halves, Fancy-Dan centres and Glory-Boy goal-kickers among the inductees, and you can understand why those poor petals in the front-row union feel just a little unloved.

Not that dear old Jason will lose too much sleep contemplating the fundamental unfairness to be found at the heart of front-row forward's condition. He seldom worries about anything. Right at the start of the professional era, when I was attempting to make a sustainable living in the world of rugby magazines (fat chance!), I wrote a piece for my publication's "Heroes and Villains" section on the "Phantom Puncher of Barking", dealing with a mysterious incident during the 1996 Calcutta Cup match at Murrayfield in which Rob Wainwright, the Scotland captain and a player in the form of his life, found himself on the uncomfortable end of what the upper classes call a bunch of fives and, as a consequence, somewhat incapacitated. The article was accompanied by a silhouette rather than a photograph – libel laws are libel laws, after all - but it hardly required the services of a pipe-smoking sleuth from Baker Street to put a name to the shape. Jason was in touch, immediately, but not to say he would be seeing us in court. "Do you think I could have a framed copy?" he asked.

Being a 24-carat West Countryman (or should that be a 24-carrot West Countryman?) whose DNA is purest Somerset, it is entirely natural that I should not always have held London rugby types in the highest esteem. But it was hard not to get along with Jason, just as it was difficult not to enjoy the company of another of the "gor blimey" element to be found in England's World Cup-winning vintage, Lawrence Dallaglio. While scraping a wage of sorts with the aforementioned magazine, I travelled to the capital in the spring of '96 for a lunchtime rendezvous with the man who, despite being an early twentysomething, had been charged with the task of saving Wasps from the worst ravages of fledgling professionalism, which had already stripped them bare in the personnel department. We ate sausage and mash in a boozer somewhere – oh, the glamour – and struck up an excellent working relationship as a result. In the next issue, we talked up Dallaglio as a future England captain and identified a fascinating, if somewhat elusive character by the name of Clive Woodward as a national coach in waiting. A few months later, we were able to raise the bar of unbearable smugness to previously unimagined heights.

Richard Hill, who played umpteen games with Dallaglio and Neil Back in the most effective of England's many excellent back-row combinations, also springs to mind in this regard. He was not really a London type, even though he joined Saracens early and never left them. Hill was, at least in terms of his rugby upbringing, a Wiltshireman: indeed, this writer first clapped eyes on him in a schools' cup final at Twickenham, playing for Bishop Wordsworth's of Salisbury and very nearly winning them the cup single-handed. The late Elwyn Price, a Welshman with a voice like a strangulated eunuch who may just have been the best talent-spotter of the age, pursued Hill up hill and down dale on behalf of Bristol for months, to no avail. "The bastard!" he said at the time, almost choking on his half of bitter shandy. "He's going to bloody London . The best player I've seen in years and he's going to…" Elwyn being Elwyn, he could not bring himself to repeat the profanity. " London ", that is, not "bloody".

Like his 2003 brethren – Leonard and Dallaglio and Back, Jason Robinson and Martin Johnson – Hill fully merits his place among the elect; certainly he ranks among the very finest players of his generation. And it is the urge to rank and rate, common to all aficionados of this most demanding of team sports, that gives "Wallhalla" its fascination. Are all the right men present and correct? Now, there's a question.

To this writer's way of thinking, there are one or two missing links. No Os du Randt or Robert Paparemborde among the grunt-and-groaners? No John Eales or Michael Jones or Wayne Shelford? Crikey. And have there really been many better outside centres than the supremely dangerous Danie Gerber of South Africa ? Poor old John Palmer, the highly accomplished Bath midfielder whose immediate reward for a long and patient ascent to England status was a close encounter with Gerber that proved too much for mere flesh and blood to stand, might have a view on the subject. But the best of anything is always a matter for discussion, debate and disagreement. That's the fun of it.

Suffice to say that a goodly proportion of my own Stellar XV can be found among these pages. Blanco was the greatest of all full-backs, and I'll happily enter the ring with anyone who dares to suggest otherwise. Campese and Lomu? I can live with those two on the wings. Michael Lynagh? If ever I needed an outside-half to win the game that would save my life, the Queenslander would be an immediate choice. Gareth Edwards? No issues there, and I'm every bit as happy with Fitzpatrick and Johnson on the basis that no team wins a serious game of rugby without winning the fight first.

Which leaves me with two of my own special favourites: the French centre Didier Codorniou – "le petit prince", the finest passer of a ball I ever clapped eyes on – and Graham Mourie, the All

Black captain who had the inner strength and the moral stature to relinquish that most coveted of positions on grounds of conscience. It is far from certain that many of us would include either man in the team of his dreams, but it should not be forgotten that some of the rugby played by France when Codorniou was pulling the strings for Blanco, Sella and company was the stuff of beauty, or that when Mourie refused to play against the incoming Springboks on that benighted, nation-splitting tour of 1981, he had established himself as an open-side flanker of the highest calibre – one who significantly changed the way those in his position played the game.

Yet there are those of another, older vintage – even, maybe, from the pre-television era – who will see things differently because they saw a different breed of player, playing a different game. They could, and surely should, argue the case for Muller, "Die Windhond", as the finest No 8 in the annals, or for Gerry Brand as the most influential of all full-backs. In the years either side of the Second World War, the Springboks were undisputed champions of the union game, and when I first dipped a toe in the waters of sports journalism with the Bristol Evening Post, the paper's municipal correspondent (a very high-powered personage indeed) decided I was in need of a proper rugby education based squarely on South African virtues. "The 1951-52 Boks were the best side I ever saw," he told me. "Read all you can about them, for we will never see their like again. That man Muller was a titan."

The rugby enthusiast finds his titans where he may. Comparisons across time are inherently fatuous: would Muhammad Ali have beaten Rocky Marciano over 15 rounds, or Bradman's Australians seen off the West Indies of Roberts and Holding and King Viv? None of us can say. Union men of sufficiently advanced years might have sensed a little of Muller in the young Dallaglio, but they could not conclusively argue that either man would have subdued the other had they met face to face. All we have is memory and opinion, the second burnished by the first. The glory of this book is its capacity to stir, to provoke, to celebrate. Waugh might have called it "Rugby Revisited".

Chris Hewett,
Rugby Correspondent The Independent
May 2010

Preface

Twickenham's Centenary embraces 85 years of amateur rugby union, with the remaining 15 years under the banner of professionalism, but, without exception, all the players who appear on the Wall of Fame played as amateurs, with the most recent of them straddling the two eras. They all have a tale or two to tell about the Headquarters of English Rugby Union.

Of course there are a great many more fine players who could have made it on to the Wall of Fame, however, there can never be a definitive list of great sportspeople, no matter what the sport, it is too subjective an operation. For all that, there will doubtless be critics who will produce numerous lists of several hundred omissions, players who they feel should have been inducted on to the Wall of Fame. Perhaps they will be right. Then, if nothing else, this book and the Wall of Fame itself, will have accomplished something else, they will have engendered discussion, debate, argument, which in themselves indicate a healthy interest in the subject.

Anyway, the fact of the matter is that this is the list. As far as the Wall of Fame goes, an attempt has been made to record for posterity, those players who have made their mark, for whatever reason, in the game in general and who have graced Twickenham in particular with their gifts, their guts and in some cases their gumption.

There were plenty of close calls and tough decisions, so the names that do feature on the Wall have been thoroughly examined and tested for their worthiness – none has been found wanting.

The names span the stadium's entire existence, from 1910 to 2010, technically speaking 101 years, which may allow the induction on to the Wall of Fame of a 101st player, quite possibly Jonny Wilkinson. But this book has been compiled with Wilkinson still playing, and one of the criteria for induction on to the Wall is that every player has to have retired from international rugby.

On a more prosaic note, players' caps are for their country only, so British Isles and Ireland appearances are not included, although tests against the Lions by Australian, New Zealand and South African players are included in the overseas players' caps' total.

There will appear to be a great deal of inconsistency as regards length of article for the various inductees, this is owing to the fact that originally the pieces were written for match programmes and were, perforce, restricted for space; once the World Rugby Museum was able to carry them on its web-site more room was available, and was duly filled.

While the pieces appear in no particular order, there are two exceptions. The book opens with Martin Johnson, since he was, after all, voted by the public as the first among his equals on the Wall of Fame. The book closes with England's Freddie Chapman, scorer of the first try at

Twickenham, and Cliff Morgan, who once graced the playing stage with his staggering array of skills, before giving his voice to rugby with his wonderful commentaries.

Johnson, Chapman and Morgan – the first and last words at Twickenham, so to speak. And many other equally impressive ones between them. All one hundred players epitomise everything that is good about this great game.

David Llewellyn
May 2010

Martin Johnson

England Second row

Born: 9.3.1970
Caps: 84
Debut: v France 1993
Last app: Australia 2003

M artin Johnson's deeds for England and Leicester had already guaranteed him a place on the World Rugby Museum's Wall of Fame, but his place in the Pantheon of great rugby union players to have graced Twickenham during its one hundred years of existence has also been fully endorsed by the fans.

As befits England's most successful captain, the supporters voted Johnson, the former England, British and Irish Lions and Leicester Tigers captain, as the player of the century, above the 99 other giants of the world game who have played at Billy Williams' famous 'Cabbage Patch'.

But Johnson is a genuinely modest man. He could barely believe that he had been inducted on to the Wall of Fame, let alone to have been voted as the best of the best.

"Being on the Wall of Fame is a bit unreal," said Johnson, whose record as captain of England saw him lead his country to 34 victories in 39 tests, including the historic victory in the 2003 Rugby World Cup final. "You see what you have done, but then there are the names of players from history, people you never saw play, such as Wavell Wakefield, Tony O'Reilly, Coin Meads, or whoever; they are followed by the guys you grew up watching, Gareth Edwards, JPR Williams; then there were the likes of Jean-Pierre Rives, Bill Beaumont, so it does seem a bit strange to see your own name up there, next to their names."

As for being first among 100 equals, he added: "There is no way I am the best player in that collection of 100 players." In fact he puts his elevation to that lofty status down to Sydney in 2003, when England beat Australia for the fifth time under Johnson's captaincy, to become the first Northern Hemisphere team to lift the Webb Ellis Trophy.

"It was more a vote for England winning the 2003 World Cup. It is in people's memories," he said with typical pragmatism.

There is no question of his right to be named among the hundred, though, because his feats as line-out expert and leader are legion, especially at Twickenham, which is what actually matters where the Wall of Fame is concerned.

A towering presence... England's
Martin Johnson in his playing days

In 44 tests at Headquarters, Johnson, as player and captain, was on the losing side on just five occasions (Ireland 1994, South Africa 1995, France 1996, Australia 1998 and New Zealand in the 1999 Rugby World Cup), enduring two drawn tests along the way, both in the autumn of 1997, opening with a 15-15 effort against Australia, following that a week later with the famous 26-26 draw against the All Blacks.

With so many matches for club and country behind him, Johnson could be forgiven for not being able to recall all of them, but the majority of players tend to remember their debut for their club and most certainly their country, especially, as was the case here, if the match was on home turf, even if they claim it was all a bit of blur at the time.
But for Johnson, who has always managed to stand out from the crowd, it truly was a bit of a blur.

To be fair there was not a lot of material for his memory to latch on to. For a start he did not have the benefit of a week-long build-up to the match against France in 1993. Johnson had been scheduled to turn out in the A international at Welford Road the night before. Instead, 24 hours before the full England match was scheduled to kick-off at Twickenham, Wade Dooley, the former Preston Grasshoppers' lock pulled out after failing to recover from a thigh injury, so the greenhorn 22-year-old Johnson was sent for by the then England manager Geoff Cooke to partner the 6ft 10in Martin Bayfield in the second row, and he travelled down to the team hotel in Richmond on the Friday.

"I got a bang on the head after, I don't know, about twenty minutes," Johnson explained, "I was pretty much concussed, so the game is a bit hazy really. I didn't go off, I played on, but I didn't really realise that I was playing for England.

"I can remember the day before, but the day of the game, actually going there is very hazy. The thing is when you are concussed the short term memory gets affected, and having only had 24 hours notice that I was in the England team, I found it peculiar that I was actually playing. It was a very strange experience. It was a little bit like a dream, it was almost like I was watching it on TV.

"I was on automatic pilot for a bit, before I eventually came round and gathered my senses, then I realised that I was actually playing for England. But I have no recollection of half-time. None at all. In fact either side of half-time I have no memory at all." For the record (and for Johnson's benefit) England won the match by a point. In fact Johnson was aware of that, because he did recover enough to recall the final quarter of the game. "Towards the end of the game when I came round I can remember I started to win some line-out ball, but apart from that the memory is not very sharp."

Contemporary match reports did not appear to pick up on the fact that Johnson played for much of the match in a daze. He and Bayfield were credited with holding their own in the line-outs overall against the formidable pairing of Abdelatif Benazzi and Olivier Roumat. Indeed Johnson's second half performance impressed greatly, prompting one observer to remark, presciently, that his two-handed takes suggested that England had a ready replacement for Dooley, when the time came.

Dooley himself, a reluctant spectator, observed after witnessing Johnson's debut, that no England player could take his place for granted adding that the Leicester rookie's ability to win possession under pressure right at the end did much to allow England to hang on for victory. So, hazy it might have been to Johnson, but his international debut certainly made a sharp and lasting impression.

That said, Johnson's first appearance for Leicester at Twickenham, later that same season, in 1993 is truly etched in his memory. "My first Cup final in 1993 was big. We were a very young team, I was just 23, Graham Rowntree and Richard Cockerill were both 22. Neil Back played in that match and Matt Poole. The oldest players were Dean Richards and John Wells, who would have been in their late twenties."

For one thing it got the monkey off their backs of never having won a Cup since the start of the 1980s. But there is another reason he remembered the 1993 Cup final, because he nearly didn't make it to the ground. In fact at one point it looked as if he might have to spend the day of the domestic cup final, which was against Harlequins, listening to the match unfolding on his car radio.

It happened like this. "Leicester had established this tradition for the Cup final – I think the first time they ever got to a final they went down and back in one day. So from then on it was a day trip," explained Johnson.

"On this particular occasion the team bus was due to leave the ground in time to get to a hotel at Heathrow for lunch. So before heading to the ground I dropped my girlfriend off, for her to get on the supporters' coach. I then set off for Welford Road.

"Unfortunately on the way there I passed the team bus, heading in the opposite direction. In those days they used to make two stops, so I went back to the supporters' hotel, thinking they may have gone there, but not so. Instead, I learned, they had gone down the motorway, so I tried to chase them. They had gone down the M1, but I ended up driving myself down to the game.

"The players had got on the bus, and thinking everyone was there had set off – without me. They were on the motorway before they realised I wasn't on the bus and they were obviously panicking because they were a player short."

The most remarkable thing about that tale is that no one had noticed that Johnson was not with them. He is a pretty difficult man to miss, because, at 6ft 7in and 18st, the Market Harborough-born lock forward really does tend to stand out from the crowd. The good news was that he did make it to Twickenham and Johnson even managed to score a try, "...off a penalty move," he said, and Tigers beat Quins to lift the Cup. "That final was the start of a good run for us." And for Johnson. They won the cup again in 1997, although it was nowhere near as thrilling, and were it not for the fact that they triumphed, Johnson would possibly have consigned his memories of that day to oblivion. It was supposed to be the highlight of the first season of professional rugby in England, but Johnson said: "It was the worst Cup final I ever played in. We beat Sale 9-3. It was a grey, wet day at Twickenham and it was a horrendous game of rugby." At one point that season Leicester had been on for a treble of European Cup,

Domestic Cup and League, but by the time they dragged their battered bodies and minds to Twickenham, Johnson explained: "The team was mentally exhausted. We also had the Anglo-Welsh Cup and I had played something approaching 40 games." So the disappointment of missing out on the treble was not really a mystery. As Johnson said: "To win something, and the cup was still part of the club game's heritage then, was special." Probably even more so since the silverware was won at Twickenham.

That Cup final apart, in fairness, Johnson does not have indelible memories of any one, single match at Twickenham in his distinguished playing career, although his second cap for England, which was won later in 1993, when England took on a formidable New Zealand team and beat them, for the first time since 1983 and only the third time at Twickenham in the history of the fixture, does strike a chord with him. "In those days we didn't play the All Blacks very often, so that was a significant win," he said.

But in fact what sticks most in Johnson's memory is a number of matches. He explained: "Probably the sequence of games in 2002-2003. We beat New Zealand and Australia in close games and also beat South Africa." By which time of course Johnson had been appointed captain by Clive Woodward and the rugby world saw the beginnings of the remarkable effect this partnership was to have on English rugby.

New Zealand were first up, and no pushover, indeed they were pressing hard at the end and it took some sterling defence to keep them out. But thanks in part to Jonny Wilkinson, who claimed a full house of a try, two conversions, three penalty goals and a drop goal, for a personal tally of 21 points, plus further tries from Lewis Moody and Ben Cohen, the red rose prevailed over the Silver Fern. Wilkinson's feat took him past Jonathan Callard's record of most points by an individual in a match against the All Blacks.

Australia were next, just a week later. Johnson took up the narrative. "We were quite comfortable at half-time against Australia, then the ball squirted out of a ruck and Elton Flatley went about 80 yards and scored a try and suddenly we were behind, so we had to fight and we did. We won by a point."

They went on to beat South Africa quite handsomely the following week, running in seven tries."

After a brief break over Christmas it was back to victorious ways again in the Six Nations, when they extended their winning run at Twickenham to six tests, in the process achieving the 2003 Grand Slam. "The atmosphere at Twickenham throughout that sequence of games was very special," remembered Johnson.

The Grand Slam was followed up by victories over New Zealand and Australia on their own patch as England built up momentum for the 2003 Rugby World Cup. And by the time they had won the Webb Ellis Trophy Johnson's personal, unbroken, tally of victories reached 17, albeit that run was interspersed by other captains when Johnson was unavailable or rested.

By the time he retired from international rugby after the final in Sydney Johnson certainly had a great deal to look back on in his impressive career. And Twickenham featured very high in his memory bank.

He admitted that actual matches at HQ really do tend to be a blur. "Once the match kicks off you are in playing mode, and you deliberately blank out a lot of the crowd and those other personal thoughts, in order to concentrate on the game.."

But just before kick-off is definitely special for him. "That bit when you walk out on to the Twickenham pitch is one of the best bits, that moment when you walk on to the field and the adrenalin surges through you. Walking out and lining up for the anthem I always regarded that as being a bit of personal time, when you gather your own thoughts, your final thoughts, before you play."

Of course these days he is no longer a player, so is there a difference when stepping out on to the hallowed turf? "Definitely. As the manager there is definitely a difference when you come out on to the pitch. You are not having to prepare yourself mentally for the match, as you do when you are a player. As a manager you just go out and get your thoughts, it is a very different process."

And is it something he misses? "When, as a manager, you hear the anthems start, that's the bit, I would say, when you want to be back on the field, when you really miss being a player."

Throughout his career Johnson was also a frequent visitor to South West London as a member of the hugely successful Leicester Tigers sides of the 1990s and early 2000s, when they contested (and usually won) Cup final after Cup final, and when the play-offs were introduced, Premiership finals were added to the list.

Johnson remembered his Leicester forays to Twickenham with at least as much fondness as he did his England appearances there.

But in fact his first experience of Twickenham was as a young Tigers' fan. "I started watching Leicester in 1982 when I was 11 and the next year, 1983, when they got to the final, I went to Twickenham and saw them lose to Bristol. Stuart Barnes was playing at fly-half, in it and they had that big winger, John Carr who scored two tries." By then of course Leicester had created a little bit of English rugby history by becoming the first club to win the domestic knock-out cup three years in a row.

To the adolescent Johnson it must have seemed like a rugby Mecca. "My impressions of Twickenham as a 13-year-old were that it was a big green place. It was still the classic 1920s stadium, with the stands painted in that distinctive classic green; and compared to club rugby grounds around the country it would have been so much more impressive to me. And, after all, it was Twickenham. I watched England play Wales sometime in the 1980s. I don't remember much about the match, or the stadium, but I do recall the pitch was in very good nick and the grass being very long."

For the adult Johnson, the England player and now team manager, Twickenham means even more. "The first game I played in at Twickenham, when I made my England debut in 1993, the old West Stand was still in use, the new one was built a year or so later. I'm quite a traditionalist, I liked the old, wooden, creaky changing rooms. The things that have been held over from that were the individual baths and – the weather vane."

Everyone knows about the "old, wooden, creaky changing rooms" and the famous baths, but the weathervane is not so obvious. It is not so famous as 'Old Father Time' at Lord's cricket

Power player... Johnson in his more recent role as England manager

ground, but nevertheless it had not escaped Johnson's sharp eye. When the West Stand was demolished in the early 1990s, the weathervane, designed by Kenneth Dalgliesh and depicting Hermes, or Mercury, passing a rugby ball to a 20th Century player, was carefully taken down and restored when the new stand was completed. Johnson took time out from his interview to look it up on the internet to confirm to his interrogator, who had never noticed the weathervane, that it was where he said it was. If his new office in the revamped South Stand had overlooked the pitch Johnson would merely have to glance out of the window. As it was he explained he could not because: "My office at Twickenham is a new one in the south-west corner of the new South Stand. There is no view of the pitch, because it is on the exterior side of the South Stand."

Never mind, the position of his office cannot block his memory, and like the majority of his fellow inductees Johnson has fond memories of the deep baths, which still have a place in the new changing rooms, although they are strangers, it would appear, to hot water in the hi-tech age of professional rugby. Johnson had to take his mind back to the old amateur days for his own warm memories of the baths. "These days players have ice baths, but there was something nice about just dropping into your own warm bath after a game."

But there is far more to the ground than baths and the weathervane. "It's your home ground, that makes it special. It's Twickenham. The name itself is synonymous with England and English rugby. And while those green sided stands were what I would always think about as a youngster, obviously as you get older it's a lot of other things. The thing about Twickenham is that you have the whole lot. It's being on the pitch. Then there's the West Car Park brigade." Even the journey to the ground has its own special moments. "The pub in Whitton. The team bus used to drive past that pub and everyone would be standing outside it."

"Of course things have changed, even in my relatively short life, since I first went there 30 years ago. And in those days when England had just two Five Nations matches a season there, going to Twickenham, as a fan, was almost like going on a pilgrimage.

"In the 1983 Cup final there was a crowd of 33,000, which was a record back then. By the time I was playing for Leicester in 1989 the final was a sell-out, in fact in 1993, it was so popular that we had to have a ballot at work for my allocation of half a dozen tickets."

The standing of the stadium is such, in Johnson's opinion, that: "International matches there against Ireland, Scotland and Wales are like the soul of the game. They are part of the English sporting calendar, rather like the FA Cup final, Lord's test matches, Wimbledon, these fixtures are in that category of sporting events in this country. They are about tradition."

Traditionalist he may be, but Johnson still welcomes the World Rugby Museum's Wall of Fame, which can be viewed on the museum's web-site. As he pointed out: "The access to, and exposure of, modern sport is staggering.

"I grew up in a time where there was a total of four weekends of rugby on television, in the Five Nations, that was probably it for the year. Now you can watch half a dozen games in one weekend on television.

"And I like the history of rugby union. There is less film footage of those old players in the game who are on the Wall of Fame, than there is say of footballers of the same eras, so it is easy to forget those names, but those players are the ones who made rugby what it is, so it is important to preserve the memory of them on the Wall. It is frightening how quickly players are forgotten once they stop playing."

It is highly unlikely that England's own Colossus, Martin Johnson, will ever be forgotten, by team-mates, opponents or supporters of the game. However much he may play down his influence on England and English rugby he is not on the Wall of Fame for nothing. His feats have already gone down in legend. His story is a fitting start to this chronicle of the 'Greats' of a great game who have graced Twickenham with their skills and their achievements.

Bernard Gadney

England Scrum-half

Born:16.7.1909
Died:14. 11. 2000
Caps:14
Debut:v Ireland 1932
Last app:v Wales 1938

Nick Farr-Jones

Australia Scrum-half

Born:18.4.1962
Caps:63
Debut:v England 1984
Last app:v South Africa 1993

F inally a myth is exploded by a legend. Before England recorded a historic victory over the All Blacks in 1936 – the first time New Zealand had been beaten in a test in England, let alone Twickenham – it had been said that the triumphant captain **Bernard Gadney** and his team would not have cared if they had lost.

"The idea that we did not care if we lost is a load of rubbish," insisted Gadney, who, after a lifetime of devotion to the game, first as a player with, among others, Leicester and the Barbarians, then as a committee member fighting for schools rugby, had the honour of becoming the inaugural brick in the Wall of Fame at Twickenham.

"We had to be civil in defeat. One should be able to have a beer with the opposition and congratulate them on their success.

"But people who said I did not care whether we won or lost clearly did not know me. As it was we won and I can tell you we were all chuffed.

"The amazing thing was our fullback was never called on to make a single tackle throughout the match. The New Zealanders never got that far. That is testimony to the hard work our marvellous pack and the rest of the team put in."

Gadney, did have a little help from one of his closest friends, Prince Alexander Obolensky.

"Obo scored two great tries against the All Blacks," recalled Gadney, who captained the side from scrum-half. "He ran like a stag. But without the fantastic effort of the forwards in the first place, the backs would not have got the ball."

The Prince died in a flying training accident during the war, but Gadney, who went on to win 14 England caps, said: "I still visit his grave in Suffolk as often as I can, and I always try to go on Remembrance Day."

It is typical of Gadney that he should have been reluctant to single out individuals for especial mention. He sounded shocked when informed of his elevation to Wall of Fame status.

Bernard Gadney, left, with Alexander Obolensky, Cardiff-bound in 1936

Wallaby scrum half Nick Farr-Jones, an inspirational and astute leader

"I do not think I am worthy of that", he said. "There are others far more deserving." He is far prouder of the fact that it was solely due to his promptings after the Second World War that ERIC was set up, the club for former England internationals, which has boasted its own room at Twickenham since the late 1940s.

But the essence of the Wall of Fame, is that it is not restricted to Englishmen. Induction to the Wall of Fame was an all-embracing honour, inaugurated in order to underline rugby union's global appeal. One essential criterion for each inductee is that each player must have made an impact at Twickenham. And Gadney was actually first equal as the inaugural nominee. Accompanying him was **Nick Farr-Jones**, who, as captain of Australia, lifted the 1991 Rugby World Cup at headquarters by beating England in the final.

In all Farr-Jones captained the Wallabies on 36 occasions, revealing himself to be an inspirational and tactically astute leader.

That 1991 Rugby World Cup triumph was sweet revenge for his previous appearance in London three years earlier when England, under the captaincy of Will Carling – his first match in charge – had inflicted a heavy 28-19 defeat on the Wallabies.

However, Farr-Jones, a law graduate, had opened his Twickenham account in the star-studded 1984 Wallaby team, with a resounding 19-3 victory over England, and overall that 1988 setback was the only blemish on Farr-Jones's record in seven tests against England.

Andy Irvine

Scotland Full-back

Born:16.9 1951
Caps: 51
Debut:v New Zealand 1972
Last app:v Australia 1982

Adrian Stoop

England Fly-half

Born:27.3.1883
Died:27.11.57
Caps:15
Debut: v Scotland 1905
Last app:v Scotland 1912

Billy Williams' Cabbage Patch, as Twickenham was known after one of the RFU committee men took the credit for discovering the site that had once been a cabbage field, was never a lucky place for **Andy Irvine**.

But it certainly was for **Adrian Stoop**. While Irvine, Scotland's dazzling fullback blessed with pace and kicking power, never once tasted victory with Scotland at English Rugby's headquarters, Stoop led England to victory in the first international match to be staged at Twickenham in 1910.

That was the first of his two matches as captain of England although his debut five years earlier found him on the losing side against Scotland at Richmond Athletic Ground. All the same his record in these traditional clashes – the oldest fixture in international rugby – does read rather better than former Scotland and Lions fullback Irvine.

"We never had much luck at Twickenham," said Irvine, thinking back in particular to 1975, when the Scots arrived looking for their first Triple Crown for 38 years.

In that match though England just managed to pip the Scots by a solitary point although the means by which England won were dubious to say the least. Irvine, who these days is managing director of a property consultant business in Edinburgh, recalled: "At one point someone kicked the ball over my head and I had a race with the England wing Alan Morley to touch it down over the line. I was convinced that he had not grounded the ball.

"These days there would have been numerous replays and a video referee, but in those days the man in the middle had the final say and he awarded England the try.

"But afterwards Morley, who was a mate of mine admitted, 'I didn't touch it down, the referee was wrong.' But that is history now."

But Irvine, who won 51 Scotland caps and made nine appearances for the British Isles and Ireland on three tours in 1974, 1977 and 1980, admitted: "Twickenham was a tough place and

Scotland's Andy Irvine, blessed with pace and a great kicking ability

the atmosphere was amazing. The old stands were right up to the pitch-side and it was quite intimidating. It was also one of the noisiest stadiums. It was not a good ground for me when I was in Scottish colours that's for sure.

"I did OK for the Barbarians and the British and Irish Lions when we played there in 1977 for the Queen's Silver Jubilee, but the best we did in my time down there was a draw in 1979."

The other thing about Twickenham that Irvine was uncomfortable with was the pitch. "Because there were so many matches going on at the ground with the Inter Services tournaments and Harlequins among others they used to let the grass grow really long so that it would take more wear I suppose.

"But an airy-fairy back such as myself used to prefer hard, dry grounds so that I could use my pace, which Twickenham did not encourage."

He didn't do too badly though and his tally of 273 points for Scotland and a further 28 for the Lions stood as a world record for five years after his retirement from the international stage before Australia's Michael Lynagh overtook him in 1987.

Irvine would have got on well with Stoop, after whom Harlequins named their stadium just across the A316 from Twickenham.

He is credited with reconstructing English back play at the start of what came to be known as The Stoop Era.

Adrian Stoop, right, an early mover and shaker in the game

Stoop, the product of a Dutch father and a mother of Irish and Scottish stock, was brought up in a large house in West Byfleet in Surrey and attended Rugby School before going up to Oxford to read law.

It was while playing for the Dark Blues that Stoop first began to develop his ideas of back play, looking for more inter-action among the halfbacks and centres. His approach was only fully developed after he had left Oxford, when he played for Harlequins and England, finally giving up as a scrum-half and settling down as an outside half, from where he could direct his backs more readily.

Stoop was a gifted player, blessed with balanced running and what has been described as exceptional speed off the mark. But his great strength lay in his ability to read a game, to think on his feet. He was always prepared to switch an attack. And he could thrill a crowd. Even when captaining Oxford in the 1904 Varsity match, which the Dark Blues lost, he had brought the crowd at Queen's Club in Kensington, to its feet with a 50-yard sprint through the massed Cambridge defences for one of the great solo scores of the fixture to date.

But it was his stunning response to the kick off of the first match on Billy Williams' former Cabbage Patch, aka Twickenham, for which Stoop will forever be remembered.

No more dramatic opening to the ground's inaugural match, which was against Wales, could have been staged. Benjamin Gronow had the honour of kicking off – the start had been delayed by a quarter of an hour because of traffic congestion.

Stoop caught the ball, but then, instead of the expected kick into touch, which was the standard response in those days, the unconventional and inventive Harlequin player, opted to run the ball.

He swung left into the Wales half. A loose scrum formed, Stoop received the ball from that and fed Cornish centre Barney Solomon, who found fellow centre John Birkett and the ball ended up in the hands of Frederick Chapman and the winger touched down for the first try at Twickenham. England went on to win the match.

Stoop, having distinguished himself on the playing fields of Europe, then covered himself with glory on the battlefields of Mesopotamia, winning the Military Cross as a Lieutenant in fifth Battalion, the Queens (Royal West Surrey) Regiment for "... conspicuous gallantry and devotion to duty in action ..." in the campaign to capture Ramadi from the Turks. He was injured, shot in the groin, but carried on fighting and then spent two months recuperating. He was promoted to captain and in the summer of 1918 the award of his MC was gazetted.

Stoop, who eventually became the president of Harlequins, also gave distinguished service to the Rugby Football Union, becoming president in the early 1930s. He had also been party to Quins' tenancy of Twickenham.

Gary Armstrong

Scotland Scrum-half

Born: 30.9.1966
Caps: 51
Debut:v Australia 1988
Last app:v New Zealand 1999

Peter Brown

Scotland Second row

Born:16. 12 1941
Caps: 27
Debut: v France 1964
Last app:v Presidents XV 1973

Twickenham is a special place, that is the long and the short of it as far as two legendary Scotland players, **Gary Armstrong** (5ft 9in) and **Peter Brown** (6ft 4in) are concerned.

The pair of them have mixed memories of the ground, but the stadium still has a special place in the memories of both men.

They are at each end of the scale, agony and ecstasy, as far as experiences go at Billy Williams Cabbage Patch. Sadly Armstrong never tasted victory on the ground, although under his captaincy in 1999 Scotland got dangerously close to a win, and in his first appearance there the Scots forced a 12-12 draw.

"In general my memories of Twickenham are of us leaving the ground with tail between legs," said a rueful Armstrong.

"But there was always a great atmosphere at the ground, even before the redevelopment. And you have the car parks filled with posh cars and the boots of those cars filled with champagne, as opposed to cans of beer. A Twickenham match is just a great occasion."

It is an entirely different tale for Brown, well almost. He had to suffer defeat on his debut there in 1965 and that turned into a double on his next visit to South West London four years later, when again Scotland lost.

But when second row Brown returned as the captain in 1971 that all changed on the team and the personal front. Little wonder then that his view of Twickenham is that the place was stimulating for the away side as well as the home team: "It certainly did not intimidate us."

That was proved in emphatic fashion on a March day in 1971, when Brown played a key role in an electric climax to the match.

The Scots were trailing 11-15 – Brown having contributed a try, one of three that he scored for his country in a career spanning ten years and embracing 27 caps (an impressive tally in those days when there were far fewer tests) – when centre Chris Rea made a wicked break and touched down to the left of the posts.

Twickenham nearly man, Scotland scrum-half Gary Armstrong

The score, Scotland's third try of the game, meant that Scotland just needed the conversion to record their first victory at Twickenham since 1933.

The kicker was a certain Peter Currie Brown. The fact that he was a forward, while not unique – Wales had employed, first hooker Norman Gale in the 1960s, then Allan Martin, a lock, the following decade, as principal kicker, while England had occasionally turned to Northampton second row Peter Larter (who lined up opposite Brown in 1971) to put the boot in – certainly singled him out as something of a rarity, but there was a further unusual thing about Brown. Unlike many specialists in those days who were known as toe-punters, kicking the ball using the toe of their kicking boot, Brown was a 'round-the-corner' kicker, using (in his case) his right instep to make contact with the ball, just like footballers.

Then again that should come as no surprise, since he played a lot of soccer as a boy, and his father Jock was a Scotland international footballer and a Scottish Cup winner with Clyde in 1939.

But back to Twickenham on March 20 1971, and the seconds ticking away. This was a real pressure kick for Brown, the difference between joy and despair. A chance to create a little bit of Scottish rugby history. With the crowd noise and the knowledge of what faced him, his nerves should have been shredded, but Brown had broad shoulders – courtesy of his Hebridean forebears – and, much more importantly, he had been awaiting this date with destiny ever since he was knee high and first able to kick a ball.

The former Gala and West of Scotland player explained: "When we were boys our father Jock always had us practising kicking the winning penalty kicks at Wembley, in England-Scotland football matches, so it was my destiny to have to take that conversion.

"On that day in March 1971, when Chris Rea scored the try, my moment had arrived, the moment I had waited and practised for in the garden and the park at Troon, since I was a boy all those years ago."

Like all good kickers before and after him, Brown had a tried and trusted approach to every kick. It never changed.

"I always went through the same routine," he recalled. "I'd make a hole in the ground and create a tee for the ball. Then I would place up the seam of the ball exactly in line with the right hand post. Because of my kicking style the ball always had a tendency to move slightly to the right, before veering left. I would keep my head steady, as per the instructions of my father. Dad had also warned me not to place my non-kicking, left foot, too near the ball, because that would cause you to miss the kick."

He followed the instructions and went through the routine and was rewarded. The ball sailed between the uprights and Twickenham fell silent for a long moment, before the Scottish supporters in the huge crowd awoke to the fact that they had just witnessed Scotland's first post war victory over the 'Auld Enemy' at English HQ.

Apparently it took a while for it to sink in with Brown as well. "At the time I didn't realise what I had done," he said modestly.

But anyone with half a belief in portents, signs and omens, would have realised what was on the cards if, like the Scotland team, they had been in London's West End the night before the match.

In those days it was not unusual for a team to go out on the town a little and perhaps have a pint or three. But Brown, who revealed that he never took alcohol throughout his playing days, went with a team tradition on that particular Friday night.

"We always went to a show the night before a match. And in 1971 we decided to go to see Pyjama Tops, at The Whitehall Theatre just off Trafalgar Square."

Pyjama Tops is not to be confused with the more proper Pyjama Game at the same venue. Pyjama Tops boasted the porn star Fiona Richmond in the lead role of a play with a plot as thin as consommé. The father of a family no longer found his interest aroused by his wife, so a string of women had to try to do what Viagra has been doing for 21st Century man.

And the dénouement sees a number of women clad only in pyjama tops coming down a staircase on to the stage, but there is a difference when the last woman appears, as Brown explained: "The last woman to come down the stairs was the French au pair."

And to the delight, astonishment and disbelief of the Scotland team members: "She was wearing a Scotland international rugby jersey, the real thing," said an incredulous Brown. It has to be remembered that this was in the days when there were no replica Rugby jerseys.

Brown continued: "The sight of that young woman in the Scotland jersey was an inspiration to us all." They took it as a sign for the following day.

In fact it was also carried over to the following weekend up at Murrayfield, when the two sides met again as part of the RFU Centenary celebrations. This time there was no nail-biting about it, the Scots recorded a thumping 26-6 victory, with Brown scoring another try and landing a penalty to boot.

But back to Twickenham, and although a generation separates the two inductees on to the World Rugby Museum's Wall of Fame, both Gary Armstrong and Peter Brown have clear recollections of the visitors' changing rooms there.

"I always looked forward to getting into the baths afterwards," said Armstrong, "you didn't get anything like those baths anywhere else. They had four or five individual baths and showers and it was good. And the pitch was always well looked after."

Brown too remembered the visitors' changing room and their luxurious facilities. "The baths at Twickenham were very interesting. There were five in the visitors' changing room, as I remember, and after a game there was always a lot of horseplay among our team members in those baths."

Brown's thoughts also stray back to getting on to the pitch before a game. "A memory that has stayed with me about Twickenham was the way you came out of the tunnel," he said. "You went down to a level below the pitch, then you had to go up rickety wooden stairs to get on to it."

Naturally Brown is happy to remind England fans: "And for a kicker it was a good place because the posts showed up very clearly against the background at each end. The last time I played for Scotland was at the Parc des Princes in Paris and I found I couldn't make out the posts when I was setting up a long range kick."

The atmosphere at the ground, in particular before the redevelopment took place many

visiting players found themselves at times uncomfortably close to the spectators and the noise was deafening.

Brown admitted: "The old Twickenham was never quiet. The noise was fantastic, all-encompassing. But that cacophony inspired you to play."

His views are echoed by Armstrong, who said: "It was always nice to try to silence the crowd, although that was a bit difficult at times."

Perhaps it was difficult because not only were they playing away, but Calcutta Cup matches always seem to have an edge over fixtures. As Armstrong said: "When Scotland meet England form goes out of the window." He feels there is a weight of history, one that presumably transcends the boundaries of sport and ventures into the many bloody battles that have been fought between the two countries over the centuries.

"I think when Scotland play England, no matter what the sport, there is something else added to it. It is always a big thing and it goes back a long way," concluded Armstrong.

At least in retrospect these two legends of Scottish Rugby can look back on their Twickenham experiences with fondness, all trace of traditional cross-border enmity, buried. Brown gets the last word on the Stadium that he and Armstrong graced with courage and honour: "These days Twickenham is a terrific stadium."

Both men confessed to feeling hugely honoured at their induction to the World Rugby Museum's Wall of Fame, although Armstrong could not resist a gentle quip. "It is not often you get such recognition from the English. All I had ever had out of the English at Twickenham was that draw." There again, it is a rare treat to have such magnificent players as Armstrong and Brown and the rest of the inductees, gracing this hallowed plot.

Neil Back

England Wing forward

Born: 16.1.1969
Caps: 66
Debut: v Scotland 1994
Last app: v Australia 2003

There is a symmetry to **Neil Back's** representative rugby career. It began and ended with Australia. He finished on a high against the Wallabies, as a member of England's World Cup-winning team in 2003.

However, he had a less than auspicious beginning. His first representative match was against Australia Schoolboys back in 1987. It was a match England lost, but defeat was sweetened by the fact that the match was played at Twickenham, a rare treat since it was usually the domain of the senior sides and of course Harlequins at the time.

His memory of his first steps on the hallowed turf of headquarters is limited to the on-pitch activity. He cannot remember if the crowd was big. Can't even remember much about the stadium.

"A match is not about the crowd," explained Back. "Even in those days I walked the edge of the pitch and looked in, towards it, everything else before, and during, a game is nothing but hype and distraction."

Anyway he already knew what the place looked like. "I'd been there before to watch a Varsity Match, although I had not watched an international.

"But playing there was a great occasion for a schoolboy. It was an unbelievable experience to play my first representative match at Twickenham."

It is youth, indeed infancy, and the Twickenham connection that has somehow struck a chord with Back ever since then. So much so that in the 1999 Rugby World Cup, after England had beaten Italy by a cricket score, Back carried his then new-born daughter Olivia, aged six days, around the England dressing room afterwards.

As introductions to the game goes it wasn't a bad one, four years later Olivia was once more in the company of Back and his England team-mates, this time in Sydney's Telstra Stadium; the tiny talisman was kissed, hugged, held aloft and generally enjoyed as much as the trophy itself.

Not long after his schoolboy debut on the ground Back found himself back there, in 1990, a step closer to his ambition of playing for his country – but this time in opposition to England as a member of the Barbarians back row.

Best foot forward as ever... England flanker Neil Back

"That was a fantastic experience," he said. "I got on the pitch for the last 25 minutes and I was involved in one of the tries, which Phil Davies scored in a corner after a back row move. That appearance put me on the map at senior level.

"It was an incredible experience for me. I remember going into the players' dining room and sitting alongside one of the world's greats David Campese and I felt out of my depth and a bit guilty that I was a part of it all. I had got in as the uncapped player but I took it all in."

Sadly the England selectors did not. His 25 minutes went unnoticed for a further four years. There were various reasons given for his exclusion, one of the chief ones being his lack of height as an openside flanker.

It was not until the 1994 Calcutta Cup match at Murrayfield that Back finally pulled on a Red Rose jersey to make a victorious debut, albeit by a single point.

A fortnight later he was back at Twickenham, this time as a senior England player to take on Ireland. They lost, coincidentally by a single point. "Myself and four others were dropped after that game," said Back, who would have to wait a further three years before returning to Twickenham. "It's not a great memory of Twickenham, that Ireland defeat."

There was an even more unpleasant memory two years later, in the 1996 Pilkington Cup final between his club Leicester and Bath.

The Tigers lost the match late in the game when referee Steve Lander awarded Bath a penalty try. When the whistle blew a disappointed Back pushed out blindly in anger at a figure in front of him.

Unfortunately that figure was Lander. The match official fell over and Back was subsequently banned for six months.

"I regret it now, but I am a very competitive person. And contrary to what was said in certain quarters I did not run after the official. He walked across my path and I pushed at a body, in frustration, it could have been anyone, even one of my own team-mates, but it happened to be Steve Lander."

But every cloud and all that. Back, who has a reputation as a fitness fanatic, took advantage of the lengthy ban. "That six-month break from playing allowed me to refresh myself. I got myself together. In that time I got engaged to Alison, bought a house and had a month off, then I used the next five months to get myself fit."

Finally he was back at Twickenham, starting in the back row against New Zealand, having appeared in the first test at Old Trafford in Manchester a week earlier, and while not tasting victory, Back at least did not finish on the losing side, rather he found himself a part of English rugby history by playing in the first – and to date the only – draw between the two countries.

It was all brighter after that. Indeed some of his proudest moments in an England shirt at Twickenham came in 2001 when he was asked to captain his country.

"I captained England against Australia," he explained, "and we beat them 21-15 and I lifted the Cook Cup on behalf of England. That was one of my proudest moments."

That was the first of a total of four matches in charge and Back can boast a 100 per cent record. He was captain when England raced to their record 134-0 victory over Romania. That annihilation came a week after the walloping of the Wallabies.

"We beat Romania to nil," said Back, "which was important to me. I wanted us to be totally ruthless and we were. We really nailed them that day." His final match in charge was the following season against Italy in Rome and coincided with the winning of his 50th cap. More significantly, a week earlier he had led England to a crushing 50-10 victory over Wales at Twickenham.

Now, with 66 caps to his name and a place in the pantheon of great England players, Back is almost lost for words at his elevation to the Twickenham Wall of Fame. "I find it incredible that I am included in such an illustrious list of players.

"I feel very privileged. It is a fantastic honour." Back can now walk tall into English, and world, rugby history.

Bill Beaumont

England Second row

Born: 9.3.1952
Caps: 34
Debut: v Ireland 1975
Last app: v Scotland 1982

Jackie Kyle

Ireland Outside half

Born: 10.1.1926
Caps: 46
Debut: v France 1947
Last app: v Scotland 1958

There have been three misses in **Bill Beaumont's** life, and he ran up against all of them at Twickenham. The first miss was at the start of the 1980 Grand Slam season, coincidentally against Ireland (who began the match as favourites for the championship); the second involved a refereeing oversight when the wrong ball was used to score a try against England; the third miss was Erika Roe, who made an unscheduled appearance at half time in the 1982 test against Australia.

Of that first miss, Beaumont said: "It came about because I did not know where the try line was. I remember it was towards the end of the match, I was tackled by Colin Patterson – at 5ft 5in the smallest guy in the pitch – just a yard short. Had I known I was that close to the line I would have driven through the tackle and scored, instead I turned to present the ball to the supporting players. That was the closest I ever got to scoring in an international."

That Beaumont almost missed seeing the topless Erika can be put down to his dedication as captain. He was giving his earnest half-time pep talk when he suddenly became aware that the rest of the team's minds and eyes were elsewhere, following the progress of the topless Miss Roe. "I was standing on the halfway line looking in one direction and the other 14 guys were looking straight through me or over my shoulder," Beaumont recalled in his autobiography *Thanks to Rugby*. "Great mates like Smithy (Steve Smith) and Brace (Peter Wheeler) were ignoring every word I was saying. Eventually I looked around to see what the distraction was – or should I say were? I must admit it was a fantastic sight."

In between those came the one against France in 1981. "It was the final game of the Five Nations," explained Beaumont, whose career ended prematurely at 34 appearances after he was ordered to retire on medical grounds in 1982. "France were going for the Grand Slam. Our fullback, Marcus Rose, kicked the ball high into the old West Stand; it probably landed in the Royal Box. Their scrum-half Pierre Berbizier immediately got hold of another ball, they took a quick throw-in and scored their first try.

A big hit and some misses… Bill Beaumont, England's 1980 Grand Slam captain

An enduring legend, Ireland's mercurial outside half Jackie Kyle

"My dear friend on the International Board, Allan Hosie, was the referee and I made a couple of comments at the time to him about him missing the fact that the French had used a different ball, but in truth they deserved to win that day."

Now, some 20 years on from that hat-trick of misses Beaumont, along with Ireland's legendary fly-half and former captain **Jackie Kyle**, has been voted a hit.

Kyle, who held the record for most Ireland caps (46) by a stand-off for a long time until overtaken by Ronan O'Gara, was a member of the team which completed the Grand Slam for the first time in Ireland's history, in 1948. Appropriately that Grand Slam was completed at Ravenhill, in Kyle's home city of Belfast in March of that year.

In that triumphant season Kyle scored a try in the narrow victory over England at Twickenham, before going on to play a crucial role in their championship-winning team the following year.

Kyle won an army of fans Down Under when he won six British Isles and Ireland caps on the 1950 Lions tour of New Zealand and Australia. He retired from international rugby to pursue a medical career in 1958, working overseas, before returning to settle in Co Down in his retirement.

Fran Cotton

England Prop

Born: 3.1.1947
Caps: 31 caps
Debut: v Scotland 1971
Last app: v Wales 1981

Hennie Muller

South Africa No.8

Born: 26. 3 1922
Died: 26.4.1977
Caps: 13
Debut: v New Zealand 1949
Last app:v Australia 1953

He might not have played in a full-blooded test on home soil against South Africa, but **Fran Cotton** did lock horns with one or two of their legendary figures at Twickenham.

It was the occasion of the iconic prop's third cap for England. The Rugby Football Union was celebrating its Centenary in 1971 and the 23-year-old Loughborough Colleges tighthead found himself lining up against some serious rugby legends.

"There was Colin Meads for a start," recalled Cotton. "Possibly New Zealand's greatest forward ever. And he was paired in the second row alongside Hannes Marais, a superbly talented South African lock. For 15 minutes that was probably the finest second row pairing in the world, unfortunately Meads injured his back after a quarter of an hour and had to leave the field."

Cotton is an unashamed admirer of Springbok rugby. He subsequently toured the Republic a year later under the captaincy of John Pullin. "Micky Burton was picked at tighthead for the test, but it was an incredible experience. My lasting impressions of South African rugby are and always will be, of brown playing fields, sunshine, full houses and a dynamic style of play."

Cotton has been something of a nemesis to the Boks whether playing them, watching from the stand or managing their opponents. England won the 1972 confrontation, two years later as a 1974 British and Irish Lion, Cotton shared in the stunning series win, taking part in the infamous '99' call from captain Willie-John McBride which saw the tourists getting their retaliation in first against a very physical side and mixing it with their opponents in a brutal third test.

Later Cotton managed the 1997 Lions tour to South Africa which resulted in a series win for the tourists. But back at Twickenham in 1971, the Springboks in that President's XV enjoyed a special moment – victory against a side that included Cotton.

It was his third defeat on the trot in an England shirt, but Cotton's worst memory of headquarters came in 1982, just after he had retired. He was heading for the home dressing

Glorious mud... England's Fran Cotton forever in the thick of the action

'The Greyhound'... South Africa's explosively quick forward Hennie Muller

room to congratulate his close mate Steve Smith on leading England to victory over Wales – a rare thing in those days.

"Bob Weighill, who was secretary of the Rugby Football Union at the time, stopped me and asked me where I was going. I told him I was off to the England dressing room to congratulate my former team-mates. But he said, 'Sorry you're not allowed in there.' I was so upset. It was, and still is, my worst moment at Twickenham."

But he has also had some great moments, including the matches there on the way to the 1980 Grand Slam and his fondness for the ground is evident when he calls to mind that the French refer to Twickenham as 'The Cathedral of Rugby'. Now the game's icon can rightfully take his place in that very cathedral after being elevated to the Wall of Fame.

His co-inductee, the late Hennie Muller, is another deserving of this signal honour. Muller, credited with being the fastest forward ever to have worn the Springbok jersey, at least until

Pierre Spies rocketed into the 21st Century, was nicknamed 'Windhond', which translates as 'Greyhound'. Muller captained South Africa to a Grand Slam of wins over the four Home Countries and France in the 1951-52 tour of Europe. A feat not many achieve. Muller, who won 13 caps in the Springbok back row, tasted defeat just once, against Australia the following season. He was a ferocious tackler, something of a human wrecking ball, and was possessed of devastating speed off the mark, which invariably enabled him to reach attackers before they had time to use the ball. He was able to nullify countless attacks against New Zealand when they toured South Africa in 1949.

On that 1951-52 tour the Springboks arrived at Twickenham with three Home Nations scalps to their name, a thumping 44-0 victory over Scotland, a handsome 17-5 win against Ireland, and a more prosaic 6-3 defeat of Wales. Muller had taken over the kicking duties from the prop Aaron 'Okey' Geffin, converting their only try scored in the first half of what was by all accounts a dull match. Their outstanding scrum-half Fonnie Du Toit had made the touchdown which saw the Tourists reach half-time with a slender two-point lead. Muller then made victory safe with a second half penalty, the ball going over the crossbar with help from a post. Muller and his men then headed for Paris where they hammered France 25-3. However they were not undefeated on the tour, London Counties having beaten them early on, but that one blemish could not detract from their overall achievements, as they won 30 out of 31 matches on the tour. In fact Muller only tasted defeat once in his brief test career, that was against Australia at Cape Town the following year, 1953, when the Wallabies won 18-14, although the Boks took that series 3-1.

Bob Hiller

England Fullback

Born: 14.10.1942
Caps: 19
Debut: v Wales 1968
Last app: v Ireland 1972

Gerry Brand

South Africa Fullback

Born: 8.10.1906
Died: 4.2.1996
Caps: 16
Debut: v New Zealand 1928
Last app: v British and Irish Lions 1938

The shock waves would have been felt throughout the rugby world when the former Northampton flanker Don White was appointed coach – coach mind you – of the national team.

Gins went down the wrong way in committee rooms around the country. But greater splutterings followed when it was learned that as part of the campaign to ensure a first England victory over South Africa in those dark days of 1969, it was decided that a squad of 30 players be selected four months before the December date, rather than the usual naming of a team in the week of the match.

Bob Hiller, the Harlequin fullback was a member of that squad and the captain, his first time at the helm. He was also puzzled. "I don't know what prompted the change in approach," he said. "Nor who was behind it, Micky Steele-Bodger maybe, or Albert Agar, who took over from Micky around that time as chairman of selectors.

"We had been used to a run-out on the Friday before a match. And when Thursday afternoons were added to the build-up we were expected to pay our expenses to training sessions.

"But this time we had to go to Leicester to train under a coach. Don was England's first proper coach. This was really professional stuff."

But if any committee buffer doubted the wisdom of the change of policy they were soon disabused of the notion. The squad practice sessions, while perhaps not making perfect, certainly helped to create a bit of English rugby history. Tries by Peter Larter and John Pullin, the latter converted by Hiller shortly before he left the field injured, plus an earlier penalty by the England captain, ensured a historic victory.

"It was fantastic when the final whistle went," recalled Hiller. "In those days England met New Zealand and South Africa so infrequently that a player was lucky to have one cap against each in his career. It was very emotional afterwards."

As for his injury, Hiller explained: "It was the first time I had ever left the field injured. I

An early 'professional'... England fullback Bob Hiller

took a hit on my right hip; it must have hit a nerve because my leg was semi-paralysed for a while and I could not move the leg properly. The feeling finally came back when I got in the bath afterwards."

That fixture was the last time the two countries were to meet for 23 years as the anti-apartheid protest finally hauled sport into its all-exclusive circle.

Hiller said: "There had been protests throughout the tour and although it had little or no effect on us I am sure it unsettled the Springboks."

The reaction of Hiller, a schoolmaster, to his elevation onto the Wall of Fame was typically modest. Hiller, a rugby and cricket Blue at Oxford in the Swinging Sixties, who won a total of 19 caps for England and went on two Lions tours, in 1968 and 1971, confined himself to: "It is a great honour. I am just glad to be remembered".

South Africa's legendary fullback **Gerhardt 'Gerry' Brand** was a member of Bennie Osler's 1931-2 Springboks to tour the United Kingdom and Ireland. He helped to secure a remarkable victory at Twickenham with one of the longest drop goals ever recorded, measured at 85 yards from point of kick to landing. Brand caught a clearance kick and then from out on the right-hand touchline launched the ball into legend. That kick was one of just a handful of highlights in what is widely regarded as a dull match, which was won 7-0 by the Springboks.

Although he had made his international debut in 1928, that 1931-32 tour was to establish Brand as one of South Africa's greatest players.

He was a neat man in appearance, to the point of fastidious. Contemporary observers recall him dusting down his shorts after pulling off a tackle, and many claim his white shorts were seldom soiled during a match. While fullback was where he played most, there were those among his playing colleagues who felt that Brand was equally as good on the wing.

His prowess with the boot was unquestioned. He was a forerunner of the Jonny Wilkinson school of dedicated kicking practice, spending hours working on place kicks and punts. Although a natural left-footer, Brand could kick equally well right-footed. He used to launch the most enormous touch-kicks and there were few, if any, to equal him for kicks at goal and drop kicks.

Budge Rogers

England Wing forward

Born: 20.6.1939
Caps: 34
Debut: v Ireland 1961
Last app: v Wales 1969

Philippe Sella

France Centre

Born: 14.2.1962
Caps: 111
Debut: v Romania 1982
Last app: v England 1995

Longevity links, yet separates as well, the playing careers of **Derek Prior 'Budge' Rogers** OBE and **Philippe Sella**, underlining the difference between the modern era and the mid-20th Century in stark fashion.

For years Rogers, a charismatic player whose career spanned almost a decade between 1961 and 1969, was England's most capped flanker with 34.

Sella, France's legendary centre, racked up a one-time world record 111 appearances for France in 13 seasons of international rugby, a figure which illustrates perfectly that there is far more test rugby played these days than hitherto.

Sella's mark was recently passed by Australia's scrum-half George Gregan, who has won 134 Wallaby caps.

Rogers' early memories of Twickenham are mixed. Billy Williams 'Cabbage Patch' was the setting for the final England trial, Rogers, who went on to become President of the Rugby Football Union in 2001, had been selected for The Rest versus England, and he was up against one of the shrewdest and most talented running fly-halves the Red Rose has spawned – Richard Sharpe.

"In those days the big confrontation was the one between the openside wing forward and the opposing fly-half," explained Rogers.

"But for whatever reason, I actually got the better of Sharpey that day and in fact he and The Rest's fly-half Bev Risman swapped sides and I did not do too badly against him, and there could not have been a better test for me, to take two highly talented, but very different outside halves."

It was a performance that certainly pleased the selectors and kick-started one of the more distinguished England playing careers.

He made a try-scoring debut against Ireland in Dublin in 1961, although England lost that match and followed that up with his first experience of Twickenham in an England shirt in a 5-5 draw with France in the February of that year. Victory at headquarters finally arrived on his

England's Budge Rogers, who made a try-scoring debut

second appearance on the ground in the Calcutta Cup match when England beat Scotland 6-0.

But the Bedford flanker's next appearance there, against Wales in 1962, was a doubly painful experience.

"That 1962 match against Wales was dire and finished up a 0-0 draw. The weather was just awful, so the pitch was a mud bath. Then you had Dickie Jeeps and Clive Rowlands the two scrum-halves, who spent a lot of the match kicking the ball into touch.

"But on the rare occasions that Rowlands did pass the ball I would clobber Alan Rees, the Wales fly-half, while Haydn Morgan, their flanker, took care of our fly-half Richard Sharpe when Jeeps passed the ball out to him.

"Then in the very last minute I got clear and chipped over Kel Coslett, the fullback who went to Rugby League and he late shoulder-charged me – today it would have been a certain penalty try – to such an extent that it dislocated my AC joint, the acromio-clavicular joint or collarbone. At which point the whistle went.

"And as the National Anthem was played I was lying prostrate on the ground, recovering from this clattering. And it finished up a draw when it should have been an England victory.

"As a result of that injury I missed my only game in about four years against Scotland. I had recovered from the dislocation and I played for Bedford against Harlequins and John Willcox, the Oxford University and England fullback, lifted me in a tackle, I went down on my elbow and the AC joint went out again. So that was a really memorable game at Twickenham."

It wasn't all bad though. After an unhappy spell of four matches captaining his country in 1966, Rogers was reappointed to lead England three years later when a France side featuring four new caps, visited Twickenham. It was something of a historic outcome.

His appointment as captain was a last minute thing. Dick Greenwood had injured himself playing squash the night before, so Rogers stepped in. It was his 32nd appearance for England and meant that he broke Wavell Wakefield's record of 31 caps which had stood for 42 years.

England had scored only three tries in their previous eight games against France, but on this occasion they doubled that tally under Rogers' leadership, with tries by wingers Rodney Webb and Keith Fielding and another from No8 Dave Rollitt.

The victory contributed to France's slide from Grand Slammers to Wooden Spoonists in the space of a season.

Rogers retained the captaincy for two more matches, the victory over Scotland and the defeat against Wales in Cardiff. By then he had won a record 34 caps.

Rogers' Twickenham experience was ultimately and overall, good. "There was always a wonderful atmosphere at Twickenham. By today's standards it was so intimate in a way. The spectators were closer to the action, the stands were higher.

"And it never ceased to be a huge thrill to run out on to the pitch there. There were some really good games there over that period. We had a wonderful match against Ireland in 1964, when I scored a try." Sadly England lost the game, but they contributed to a great spectacle.

Throughout his career Sella was a prolific try-scorer, although he set up many more than the 30 he scored himself, and he marked the 1986 season by scoring in all four Five Nations Championship matches, a feat that had been achieved at that time by only two other players, Frenchman Patrick Estève and England's Carston Catcheside, who managed it in his debut season 1924, when helping England to win the Grand Slam.

Sella had marked his entrance into the Five Nations Championship by scoring a try in his first match in the tournament – against England at Twickenham. It was France's third and final try of the match and the one that clinched victory for *Les Bleus*.

For six years Sella and France just could not lose against England, home or away. France had won Sella's first match against England 19-15 four years later in 1987 they repeated the feat and once again Sella got in amongst the scorers, bringing his total of tries against England to four. They were happy days at Twickenham especially for the Agen threequarter.

But as the 80s drew to a close so did the winning streak. In their next matches against England France lost every game from 1989 to 1995, and Sella remained tryless against the Red Rose outfit.

But he did have a hand in the now celebrated try in 1991, when the two unbeaten teams met at Twickenham for the Championship and a Grand Slam.

The move started behind the French posts after Simon Hodgkinson's penalty sailed wide. Pierre Berbizier caught the ball then paused debating what to do with it. Serge Blanco looped around, Jean-Baptiste Lafond took it upfield and linked with Didier Cambérabéro, who found Sella lurking like a pike in weed over on the right wing.

The centre of attention… France's brilliant Phillipe Sella who won 111 caps

The French centre held up play momentarily to allow everyone to catch up with him then he returned the ball to Cambérabéro, who chipped ahead, regathered then launched a cross kick into the middle of the pitch.

Philippe Saint-André steamed up, took the ball on the bounce and ran in under the posts. Never mind the players involved, it left the crowd breathless. It was a wonderful move to have been involved in and it serves as one simple reminder of just how great Sella's career has been.

But in case further evidence is needed, later in that same 1991 match he was at it again, this time combining brilliantly with Franck Mesnel and Blanco to conjure up another brilliant try for the former.

Ken Catchpole
Australia Scrum-half

Born: 21.6.1939
Caps: 27
Debut: v Fiji 1961
Last app: v New Zealand 1968

Jeff Butterfield
England Centre

Born: 9.8.1929
Died: 30.4.2004
Caps: 28
Debut: v France 1953
Last app: v Scotland 1959

There are distinct similarities between England's **Jeff Butterfield** and **Ken Catchpole** of Australia, co-inductees to the Twickenham Wall of Fame. Both men used their prodigious talent and skills to entertain crowds; both played a similar number of tests – 28 and 27; and both men could pass.

Butterfield the Northampton centre was renowned for – among his many qualities – his ability to off-load a perfectly timed pass to lurking team-mates.

Wallaby scrum-half Ken Catchpole was a decade or two ahead of his time in that while he eschewed the dive pass, he was possessed of a stunning delivery whose pace and perfect timing gave the receiver yards more space and precious extra seconds to do their worst.

Butterfield, who had a scorching turn of speed, played a heroic role in England's 14-man victory over Australia at Twickenham in 1958. Butterfield had moved to fly-half after Phil Horrocks-Taylor had to leave the field late in the first half of what was a brutal and bruising match.

And it was Butterfield who supplied the pass for Peter Jackson's famous match-winning try. Nine years later, the fifth Wallabies, like their predecessors also packed a hell of a punch, but of a figurative and more legitimate kind.

A key element of that force was Catchpole. He personified the philosophy of the 1967 Australians, which was to play open, running rugby. It cost them at times on that tour, but they still beat the two teams they really wanted to beat – Wales and England, the latter by a handsome margin, in fact the 23 points they amassed was the highest England had conceded on the ground since the first international at Headquarters in 1910.

That approach relied – after the forwards winning possession – on the halfbacks and threequarters employing short, sharp passes, which flew in the face of the prevailing fashion for back lines to be spread across the width of the pitch.

Catchpole's memories of the day are hazy. The Wallabies were some eleven weeks into a protracted European tour and had lost the previous test to Scotland, before Christmas.

"I remember the atmosphere in that marvellous stadium," recalled Catchpole, who was

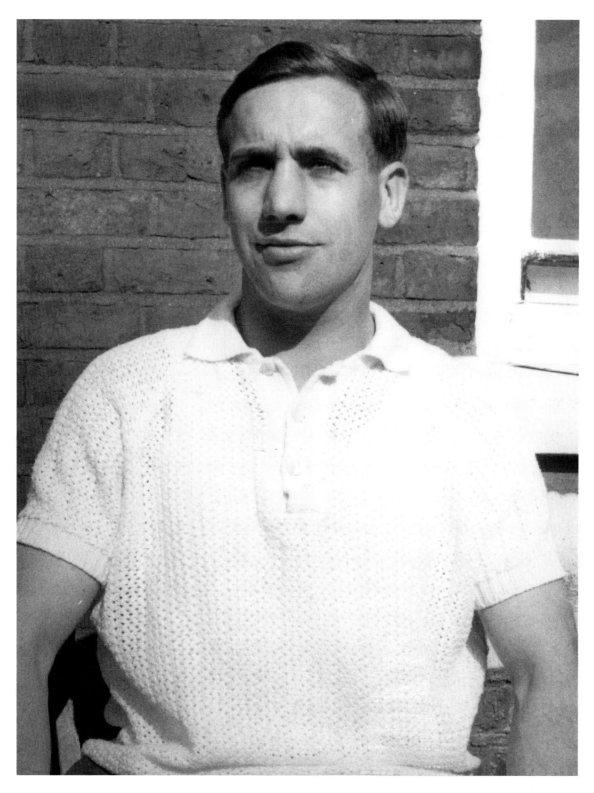

First class delivery... Australia's gifted scrum-half Ken Catchpole

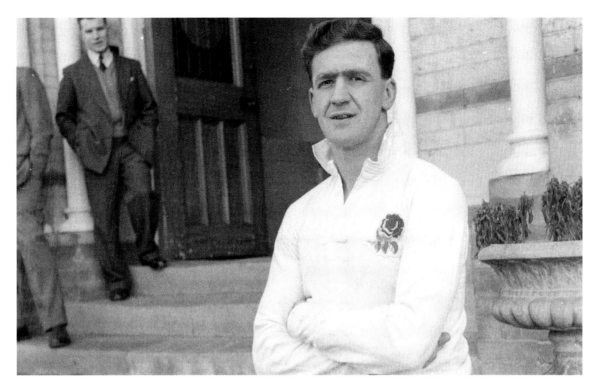

England centre Jeff Butterfield, who had a scorching turn of speed

semi-retired and a vice president of New South Wales rugby at the time of his interview, "and the enthusiasm in the stands, the front rows of which were very close to the touchlines.

"The Twickenham pitch itself was nothing like modern-day pitches. As I recall it was fairly uneven, undulating almost, but it was clearly very well looked after. As for the match, I just remember it being pretty tight and very tough. I know when the whistle went we were delighted to have beaten England."

He had to be prompted to be reminded of his late try. "I don't think it was one of my greatest tries," said Catchpole, who scored a try on debut as captain against Fiji in 1961. "I received the ball from Phil Hawthorne and the line was beckoning with scarcely any defensive cover in sight."

Hawthorne created a little bit of history in the game by scoring three drop goals, only the second player after Pierre Albaladejo of France in 1960, to achieve a feat that has since been equalled or bettered by a raft of players, but at the time stood out as something extra special. Just as Butterfield and Catchpole have done down the years. Their contributions can now be trumpeted from the Wall of Fame.

The end of Catchpole's playing career was premature. The man who captained his country on 13 occasions sustained a serious injury to a hamstring while pinned by other players at a ruck in a match against New Zealand. The damage to the muscle was so bad that nothing could be done surgically.

Chester Williams

South Africa Wing

Born: 8.8.1970
Caps: 27
Debut: v Argentina 1993
Last app: v Wales 2000

Twickenham in the autumn of 1995 was to be an important postscript in South Africa's re-emergence as a major force in world rugby.

When the Springboks squad arrived on these shores that November they did so as the reigning World Champions.

Their memorable triumph in the 1995 Rugby World Cup final when they had beaten favourites New Zealand in an emotional final at a packed Ellis Park in Johannesburg, was still fresh in the mind.

They had gone through the six matches of the tournament unbeaten, but during their storming of the world that summer there had been one notable absentee from their list of scalps – England.

By the time they landed in England their unbeaten run in 1995 had been stretched to nine games. And among their number was someone regarded as one of the most lethal finishers in the world at that time.

That someone was **Chester Williams**. No one could have been more hungry for success at Twickenham. England's own back yard, especially after having been given a fright in Rome against Italy the previous week when Williams and his team-mates had found themselves trailing as they entered the last quarter of the match. Thankfully blushes were spared with a late splurge of points.

As he put it in his acclaimed autobiography 'Chester', "[Beating] England in London would be like the dessert after the main course [of the World Cup]."

South Africa were the top dogs. The team to beat. They commanded respect, or should have.

Strangely when they were 'dissed' it was a South African who wound up the Boks. Mike Catt, the England fly-half who was born in Port Elizabeth in 1971, had targeted Francois Pienaar, the South Africa captain, for criticism in the media.

One of the game's more lethal finishers… South Africa wing Chester Williams

Catt suggested that Pienaar was a limited player and an average international. Kitch Christie the South Africa coach, was appalled. He called Catt's comments a disgrace and said England would pay for them.

Even Jack Rowell, the England coach, was quoted as saying, that Catt had learned a lesson not to be that stupid ever again.

Williams himself said later in his autobiography: "It was not the wisest of comments [for Catt] to make. Kitch fired up the guys and got a bit extra out of them at training that week.

"It had been a long season, an emotionally draining one and, physically, the players had taken a beating. If some of the guys needed a spark, Mike Catt gave it to them."

And the Springboks gave it to England on a day that was supposed to have seen the home side celebrating the opening of the revamped 78,000-seater stadium.

Andy Robinson, the present England head coach, had been recalled for the match for his eighth, and last cap, six years after his previous England appearance.

Williams made it a memorable afternoon for every South African fan by scoring two tries.

Indeed had it not been for referee Jim Fleming not seeing that the winger had touched down in the first half, Williams might well have been credited with a hat-trick of tries – video replays had showed that the ball had been grounded.

But there was no doubt surrounding the second touchdown by the Western Province winger, who pounced on a wild Will Carling pass and hacked ahead to score.

After 66 minutes Williams struck again to put the game beyond doubt, this time chasing up an André Joubert chip. Phil de Glanville's try two minutes from the close could not deny the exuberant World Champions who recorded a resounding 24-14 victory. They were indubitably the best in the world and Williams had underlined his clinical finishing, which marked him out as one of the top wingers in the world.

Sadly Williams' career was disrupted by injury thereafter, but his record speaks for itself. In his 27 Tests for South Africa Williams scored 14 tries, a strike rate that puts him up there among the best in the history of the game.

Didier Codorniou

France Centre

Born: 13.2.1958
Caps: 31
Debut: v New Zealand 1979
Last app: v Argentina 1985

Raphael Ibanez

France Hooker

Born: 17.2.1973
Caps: 98
Debut: v Wales 1996
Last app: v Argentina 2007

Didier Codorniou, the brilliant France centre of the 1980s, was called Le Petit Prince (The Little Prince), while **Raphael Ibanez**, the former captain, should be known as the king of hookers, especially since he is presently the most capped hooker in the world with 98.

Together this pair embodied all that is great in French rugby. Codorniou was a shining exemplar of what centre play is all about.

In France the centre is as highly regarded, even worshipped, in just the same way that the fly-half is revered in the British Isles and Ireland. The French want their centres to be exciting, but creative; a personality on the pitch, capable of bringing a crowd to its feet with an explosive burst or a stunning pass, because ultimately the centre has to be selfless, a true hero, since, fundamentally, his job is to create tries for the other backs. And Le Petit Prince did that not only in spades, but by the bucketload.

Codorniou, the former Narbonne and Toulouse player, who formed a potent and legendary partnership with the greatest of them all, Philippe Sella, for an all-too brief 16 matches, was truly gifted.

Blessed with a wonderful pass – its timing was never less than perfect – blistering launch speed that would take him past the first line of defence (there was not a winger who could live with him in the initial and crucial 15 metres), Codorniou had great hands, fabulous distribution skills and wonderful vision, all these attributes added up to the epitome of French centres, that of a creator of tries – he scored just five for France in his total of 31 appearances.

At the time of his interview he was the socialist Mayor of the town of Gruissan and since retiring from the game in the 1990s he has been accorded one of France's highest civilian honours, the Chevalier de l'Ordre Nationale de Mérite.

But Codorniou remembered all too clearly one of his finest moments at Twickenham. It was in 1981, when France arrived looking for the Championship and, more importantly, the Grand Slam.

Les Bleus scored two tries, both in the first half. If the first was dubious because when they took a quick throw-in they used a different ball, the second was a classic. As Codorniou recalled: "My one abiding memory is of noticing, at one point in a move in the first half of the match that the left wing Laurent Pardon was free. I was still 20 metres from the line and knew I could not get there, but having spotted him out wide I managed to find him with an acrobatic pass that 'fixed' three English defenders."

The pass put Pardon clear away and he scored the try that sealed victory and 'Le Grand Chelem'. "Moments like that are special," added Codorniou. "They are the ones that mark the high points of a career."

He worked hard to develop that brilliant passing ability though. While there was innate talent, notably in the timing of his passes, they still required work, and Codorniou did the hard yards all right.

"My pass owed its efficacy to two things," he explained from the Mayor's office in Gruissan. "The first was that I put in a lot of hard work on it. It is true I also had a natural ability to pass the ball, but I had to develop the technique with a succession of coaches.

"I was always trying to improve the quality of the pass. I was incredibly keen to do well, to improve my game and this was to my advantage. I was also lucky enough that I was able to read a game well. I could anticipate things and act accordingly."

But Codorniou was no one dimensional player. He had a well-deserved reputation as a defender. If he could create tries for his team, he was also able to prevent them being scored.

Codorniou was a fierce defender and a great tackler. His diminutive physique, 5ft 7in standing on a brick and 11 stone when wringing wet, belied the ferocity of his defensive capabilities.

"I loved tackling. I was of a modest build, and invariably I found myself opposite a far bigger opponent, so I had to employ sound technique when tackling them, and that was to tackle low.

"It was very efficient, because it stopped the player, but it came at a price, because I suffered the occasional fractured cheekbone and the odd painful blow to my shoulders. These days the higher tackles do not necessarily stop a player and bring him to ground."

Observers at the time called him beautiful to watch. He was invariably credited with making his team-mates shine. Which they most certainly did at Twickenham where Codorniou shared in two victories, the one in 1981 and again in 1983, before the two teams drew two years later.

Codorniou had followed the present France team manager Jo Maso, another genius in the centre, into the Narbonne first XV, making his debut at the age of 17. "When I was a young player my idol was Jo Maso. I first played alongside him in the Narbonne team, when I was 17 years old and at the start of my career, while he was coming to the end of his."

Eventually Codorniou left his home town club in 1986 to spend a few seasons with Toulouse before returning to his beloved Languedoc Roussillon.

But he has never forgotten Twickenham. "The first time I saw Twickenham, in 1981, it struck me that it was just like a temple. A temple of rugby. There was a mystique to the place.

"I experienced a range of emotions that day. Just having the opportunity to play at

The king of hookers... France's long serving, and former captain, Rafael Ibanez

Twickenham was something special for me. At the same time we were fearful of playing at Twickenham because matches against England were always difficult. I have always had a great deal of respect for English players.

"For me Twickenham was the most beautiful stadium I ever saw and played in during my career. And the modern stadium has not lost its magic for me."

As for his elevation to the World Rugby Museum's Wall of Fame, Codorniou said: "I am immensely honoured to have been inducted on to the Wall of Fame. When I was told, I was deeply touched. I am not sure if I deserve such an honour, but I am greatly honoured to be included with some of the great names of rugby."

Raphael Ibanez had not had the time to decide quite where his future lay, he admitted it could be coaching, but he had only just retired completely from the game, after being forced to call it a day in the middle of an important season for his adopted club Wasps when he was interviewed.

But, for someone who has plied his rugby trade in one of the hardest and darkest places on a rugby field – the front row – there is a surprisingly emotional side to Ibanez. He expresses similar thoughts to Codorniou about the Wall of Fame and about Twickenham.

His reaction to being inducted on to the World Rugby Museum's Wall of Fame at Twickenham left him bowled over. "When I was told that I had been inducted on to the Wall of Fame at Twickenham I was very emotional, because it means a lot to me," said Ibanez.

And he blew aside the hundreds of years of rivalry that have existed between France and England when he added: "And for a Frenchman to be considered good enough for such an honour by his English peers is quite something.

"After all, it is your opponents who get the best out of you, that is why when I retired from all rugby, in addition to thanking all my team-mates, I also remembered to thank all my opponents. That is why I think it such a good idea to open up the Wall of Fame to overseas players at what is the home of rugby."

There is an element of the super-stardom that inevitably settles over the shoulders of today's leading sportsmen, whatever their speciality and that is reflected in Ibanez's next words, however far-fetched a comparison it may appear to be: "For me being inducted on to the Wall of Fame, it is the equivalent of Hollywood's Walk of Fame."

Somehow the Chertsey Road does not have quite the cachet of Sunset Boulevard or Hollywood Boulevard, where film stars and musicians are celebrated on the pavements, but the Wall of Fame is no less an honour.

The fact that the Wall of Fame is at Twickenham makes his membership of what will be a celebration and recognition of an elite 100 of the world's greatest players all the sweeter for Ibanez.

"When I think of Twickenham there is one game that I recall," said Ibanez. "It was the Rugby World Cup semi-final against New Zealand in 1999."

It is probably the one match every England supporter recalled with fondness and a few goosebumps as well. It was a match which saw the mighty All Blacks brought down to earth with a crash.

And there was no luck about it, the final score had a big enough margin to suggest that France had won the game convincingly, not that the sporting and sensitive Ibanez, who was captain of France that day, remembered it that way.

"That kind of game is very difficult to explain," he said. "You can't say easily why or how it happened. But it still has a special place in my heart. Of course the game was amazing.

"I think it was probably the first time that the English supporters were behind the French team. It is for sure the last time it will ever happen. This is one of the reasons why the match was so special.

"We were aware of the special atmosphere when we were out there on the pitch. What happened was, the first half we were trying to deal with the immense pressure from the All Blacks. They had started the game as favourites. In the second half initially it became a survival mission, then came this amazing comeback. The fans by then were well behind us." France won the semi-final 43-31.

But Twickenham was not always such a great stadium for Ibanez. In all he played there for France on seven occasions, and apart from the historic victory over New Zealand he tasted victory on one other occasion there. His last appearance in a France jersey on the ground was in 2007, but that was not in the Six Nations.

"I had to wait until one of my last caps before France beat England at Twickenham," he said with an air of resignation. It was the last warm-up game before the start of the 2003 Rugby World Cup.

"I suppose, after five attempts to beat England at Twickenham and finally doing so at the sixth try, at least you could say I am the kind of guy who does not give up. I returned to Twickenham so many times with my country, yet only managed to beat England once in six visits."

But Ibanez had a great deal more luck at Twickenham with his club Wasps. "The stadium was, and still is, for me something special. Over the last three years I have appeared with Wasps in three finals at Twickenham.

"My first taste of a club final at Twickenham was against Llanelli Scarlets in the Anglo-Welsh Cup, that was in 2006, my first year with Wasps. We won that match 26-10. The following year we played Leicester in the Heineken Cup final, again we won 25-9 [Ibanez scored a try]. The year after that, at the end of last season, again we played Leicester, this time in the Premiership final, a match we won 26-16."

Oddly it was when he was playing for Wasps that he found himself being affected by the atmosphere of the place. "Twickenham can be a daunting place to play, but it can also give you the edge you need to perform well.

"I had my first experience of shivers down my spine or goosebumps when we came out onto the Twickenham pitch for the Heineken Cup final in 2007. I think that was the biggest occasion for a club game. When we came out of the tunnel I know that my parents, who were in the stands, were moved to tears. It was amazing and fantastic."

The effect of the stadium on players prompted Ibanez to say: "Twickenham is a place where you want your best players on the field and you want the best performance from them. This is where the big games are played and this is where it is a test for you and for everyone. I have a special relationship with Twickenham.

"It is an intimidating place especially when you play England, and for French players this is regarded as the ultimate test of character.

"During all the games I have played at Twickenham and most of the time whatever else you bring into the game, your skills, your stamina, your speed, your strength, what you need to bring to the games at Twickenham is your heart. You have to be ready to front up when you are there."

Ibanez comes from Dax, in the South West of France, heartland of rugby – and of another sport which demands oodles of courage and an ability to front up when the going gets tough. Like it or loathe it, bull-fighting is a part of the culture down there.

Ibanez acknowledged this. "There is a bullfighting arena in Dax. It is a big arena, but when I started playing rugby, I was very pleased to find one that was bigger than that, and that one was Twickenham.

"Twickenham is like the bullfighting arena in Nîmes, which was built by the Romans, as was the arena in Dax, when you go to these places you can almost smell the history. These arenas are for gladiators and rugby players are like gladiators."

But as the steam vaporises Ibanez was also able to reflect on more gentle uses of Twickenham. "I have always been fascinated by the West car park at Twickenham, all those fans opening the boots of their cars and having drinks and food before the game. In fact the first time I went to Twickenham I couldn't believe what I was seeing, and I was ready to jump off the team coach and have a quick glass of wine with them. It would have been good for Anglo-French relations.

"Something else that I like about Twickenham was when we played our arch rivals Leicester – and of course it is easy for me to talk about these two games because we won them – before the matches I was really surprised and impressed that you could see families, where the father for example, would be wearing a Wasps replica jersey, while the mother would have on a Leicester Tigers jersey."

As for the legendary baths, Ibanez is not quite so fond of them. "The baths are impressive, but it is not good putting herself into a bath full of ice cubes. There are no hot baths in the modern game. But when you win games it is a lot easier to step into one of these baths that is filled with ice, than when you lose."

There was one memory of the ground that Ibanez, who was captain of his country on five of the seven visits to Twickenham and in all led France on 41 occasions, cherished.

"I have one other memory of Twickenham. Originally plaques were put on the walls of the tunnel recording England victories, although I think they have been removed now.

"After that victorious game against New Zealand in 1999 one of our players, I won't say who, got a felt tip pen and wrote on the wall the score between France and New Zealand that day. And as captain I was pleased to allow this to be done after such a big game."

Sadly Ibanez said: "I think it has subsequently been painted over."

That is not something that is going to happen to the records of either Didier Codorniou or Raphael Ibanez, whose exploits not only at Twickenham, but in Rugby Union as a whole, are indelibly imprinted in the history of the game. Perhaps the Twickenham authorities may feel inclined to put up a plaque to celebrate that great France win of a decade ago. It would be a huge gesture towards Anglo-French relations, as well as probably bringing a smile to the faces of all French players, past, present and future.

Cyril Lowe
England Wing

Born: 7.10.1891
Died: 6.2.1983
Caps: 25
Debut: v South Africa 1913
Last app: v France 1923

D. J. 'Dawie' De Villiers
South Africa Scrum-half

Born: 10.7.1940
Caps: 25
Debut: v British and Irish Lions 1962
Last app: v New Zealand 1970

There have been many occasions when team members have 'chaired' their captain off the field after a great performance, but rare it is when members of the vanquished team have hoisted the victors' captain on to their shoulders and carried him off the pitch.

But that is precisely what happened to South Africa's captain, **Dawie de Villiers**, after his Springbok team had beaten the Barbarians in a thrilling game at Twickenham to wrap up the 1969-70 tour of the British Isles and Ireland.

It is a moment that Dr De Villiers savours still, one of the warmer memories he has harboured of Twickenham. "I recall I was carried off by a couple of Barbarian players," said Dr De Villiers, who these days is based in Spain, working for the World Tourism Organisation, an off-shoot of the United Nations.

"It was in recognition of a marvellous match. They, and the crowd, said Goodbye to us in great style."

That was the fourth time that De Villiers had appeared at headquarters. The troubled visit had opened up at Twickenham with a game against Oxford University, which resulted in a shock defeat for the Springboks.

At the time, neither De Villiers, as captain, nor the tour party's management claimed that the anti-apartheid protests had influenced them in any way.

But 33 years later De Villiers admitted: "That was our first encounter with the demonstrators and we were psychologically ill-prepared for what happened.

"When they got on to the pitch they distracted our attention from the game. We were hypnotised by their activities."

By the time they returned to face England they were more hardened to the protestors' antics, although De Villiers said: "We were shocked when the demonstrators ran onto the field with the police chasing them. I remember one got onto the crossbar at one end and another chained himself to an upright."

He had another, equally sharp memory of the test match as well. When England hooker,

John Pullin, dived onto the ball and was awarded a try De Villiers recalled: "I got my hand to the ball first and touched it down. I have a clear memory of that."

But overall he has retained fond memories of the place and of the games there and the camaraderie engendered in all these encounters. "That is why I feel greatly honoured to be inducted onto the Wall of Fame at Twickenham."

He was inducted onto this prestigious monument along with one of England's legendary figures **Cyril 'Kit' Lowe** MC, who made his debut on the right wing against South Africa in 1913 – the start of an unbroken run of 25 appearances for his country either side of the of The Great War.

Lowe had an outstanding strike rate, scoring 18 tries in his 25 appearances, yet by modern day standards he was miniscule, weighing almost half what is accepted for a 21st century wing, tipping the scales at a risible 8½ stone and standing just 5ft 6in. He only ever tasted three defeats with England, twice against Wales and once against South Africa.

He made his debut while still a student at Cambridge University, where he won three Blues.

During the First World War he joined the Royal Flying Corps as a fighter pilot, and claimed to have shot down 30 or 31 German aircraft, although according to one source he was officially credited with downing just nine enemy planes. In addition to winning the Military Cross Lowe was also awarded the Distinguished Flying Cross.

Lowe tasted Grand Slam glory four times with England either side of the war, in 1913, 1914, 1921 and 1923. His try-scoring record stood for 66 years after he retired in 1923, until it was overtaken by another pilot and flying England wing – Rory Underwood in 1989.

Apparently Lowe was also the inspiration for a poem 'The Great Day' by P G Wodehouse, who, like Lowe, had attended Dulwich College. Lowe also excelled at athletics (he won Cambridge University's 880 yards in 1913), cricket, boxing and swimming. After his playing days Lowe, who reached Group Captain served at the RAF College Cranwell and represented the Royal Air Force on the Rugby Football Union committee and was a selector from 1934 to 1938.

David Campese

Australia Wing

Born: 21.10.1962
Caps: 101
Debut: v New Zealand 1982
Last app: v Wales 1996

Peter Jackson

England Wing

Born: 22.9.1930
Died: 22.3.2004
Caps: 20
Debut: v Wales 1956
Last app: v Scotland 1963

The England-Australia clash at Twickenham in February 1958 was not a match for the faint-hearted, although it was a feinting run which sealed victory for the home side.

It is a game that will be remembered by those who were there for 14-man England's courageous performance and for right wing **Peter Jackson's** match-winning try.

The man himself had near total recall of that score, but he also had other, less pleasant memories.

"It was one of those games. One of the Australian centres, a youngster, was a shocker and guilty of late tackling. Today he would have been sent off after the third one."

Contemporary records report a match where a large numbers of England players were either concussed or injured during a bruising 80 minutes.

Indeed England lost their fly-half, Phil Horrocks-Taylor, with ten minutes of the first half remaining. With no replacements in those days the home side had to struggle on as best they could for the remaining 50 minutes.

"There were no prisoners taken right from the kick-off," recalled Jackson. "The Australian tackles went in whether you had the ball or not. The referee never did anything about it. But we still pulled off victory by sheer determination."

Jackson was joined on the Wall of Fame by another famous, free-scoring winger, Australia's **David Campese**.

The Wallaby, the world's most capped wing with 101, scored a memorable try or two himself in his illustrious career.

But it is Jackson's score that is the focal point here. He took up the story. "There was a perception that I could only step off my right foot, it being stronger than my left," explained Jackson who won 20 caps and scored six tries for his country.

"But I was brought up as a fly half at school and our coach, Sergeant Major Bill Moore, used to get me to run up and down the length of the playing field alternately stepping off my right foot and then my left, so in fact, going in to this match I could step off either foot."

The trademark 'goose-step' of Australia's high scoring winger David Campese

A right and a left... England's elusive wing Peter Jackson

But the Australians clearly were not aware of this ambidexterity and consequently Jackson's opposite number Roderick Phelps covered for the right-footed step.

Jackson again: "So this time I went off my left foot. Phelps did nearly get me but I managed to hand him off." Jackson then rounded fullback Terrence Curley, feinting inside before stepping outside and with Phelps, having made a startling recovery, at him again the England wing dived fully outstretched and just grounded the ball over the line.

But for Jackson it was not the try that gave him most satisfaction, rather it was the spirited way that 14 men put their bodies on the line to record, against all odds, England's first post-war victory over a Dominion side.

As for Campese, who was as renowned for his scoring of verbal points as he was for his tries – he touched down 64 times in his long and fabulous career, he had been part of the superb Wallabies party that achieved a Grand Slam over the Home Unions on their 1984 tour, and he scored two tries against Scotland.

Dickie Jeeps

England Scrum-half

Born: 25.11.1931
Caps: 24
Debut: v Wales 1956
Last app: v Scotland 1962

The intensity of preparation by the modern day England teams must have some of the old guard of the mid-20th Century chuckling a little.

And if you don't believe that, just read what happened to Dickie Jeeps when he arranged a brief get-together of the England team he was captaining in a trial match against The Rest in 1962.

"It was a trial match for the team to play Wales at Twickenham the following weekend. I was determined to play. I was captain of England at the time and had been called up for the trial match, leading an England XV against The Rest," recalled the former England scrum-half.

"I wrote to all the team and I told them 'As far as I am concerned I want to play for England and I hope you are all with me in wanting to do the same.

"'If you want to play for England versus Wales we need to win this trial match. I want you all to meet at Richmond at 2.30 next Friday.'

"When Col Frank Prentice, the secretary of the Rugby Football Union, got to hear about that, I got a bollocking. A terrible bollocking. He told me, 'This is not a professional game.'

"But the get-together worked, because we won the game and I think 14 of the England trial side went on to play in the match against Wales, so you can't say it wasn't a good idea."

Preparation seemed to be a feature of Jeeps' career, sometimes intentional, other times involuntary. For example he credits an invitation match in Cornwall in which played inside the great Cliff Morgan, for his selection for the British and Irish Lions' tour to South Africa in 1955 – in the summer before he made his England debut (against Wales) at Twickenham in 1956.

"I think Cliff got me onto the party because he liked my service. The reason I had been asked to play in this invitation match was because I had played for Northampton against Cardiff and we won 22 9 earlier in the season.

"And if I tell you that the ball went into touch just four times in that match it is no word of a lie. It was a brilliant game of rugby, I was lucky, because I had a good game and of course Cliff was playing and so he saw me at first hand."

In full flight... scrum-half Dickie Jeeps launches England's backs

It was with an eye for detail and the scouts' philosophy of Be Prepared which saw Jeeps, in his first match as the England captain – coincidentally against Wales at Twickenham in 1960 – invite the stand-by fly-half Richard Sharp up the week before to Cambridgeshire for a few practice passes.

"I had never thrown a pass at Richard Sharp before," explained Jeeps, "so, on the Sunday before, he came up to see me and we practised passing in the local recreation ground. And it was just as well we put in that time because Richard actually ended up playing in the team the following Saturday after Bev Risman got injured."

Jeeps had made his debut, unsurprisingly given the way his career went, against Wales at Twickenham in 1956 in front of a crowd of 75,000. He was one of ten new caps on that cold January day. He found himself in opposition to his Lions halfback partner Morgan, who was captaining Wales. The visitors won a match that many observers at the time felt should have been won by England.

"I was dropped after that match," said Jeeps, who had to wait until the following January when he returned – against Wales in Cardiff. This time England won and Jeeps kept his place.

In all Jeeps played 24 times for his country and captained them on 13 occasions and his leadership record makes for a creditable read: played 13, won five, drawn four, lost four.

Now when he looks back at his career he recalls with fondness the old Twickenham, and, for him, its special feature. "I used to love the old baths, they were wonderful, and the home dressing room was always nice and warm."

These days he feels the modern stadium has lost something. "With the old ground the stands used to rear up perhaps 10 yards from the touchline and it was intimidating for visiting sides. It was like a fortress to us. Now it does not seem to have those same qualities."

But he does feel there is much to commend it, including the Museum's Wall of Fame, an honour of which he said he is very proud, glad that players from other generations can be remembered in such a notable way.

Diego Dominguez

Italy Outside half

Born: 25.4.1966
Caps: 2 (Arg); 74 (It)
Debut: Arg v Chile 1989;
Italy v France 1991
Last app: v Ireland 2003

John Birkett

England Centre

Born: 27.12.1884
Died: 16.10.1968
Caps: 21
Debut: v Scotland 1906
Last app: v France 1912

Italy was not on the Rugby map when **John Birkett** was amassing his 21 appearances between 1906 and 1912, which for a while made him England's record cap holder. But, by an odd coincidence, Birkett, son of Reginald and nephew of Louis and a former Harlequin, Barbarian and England centre, did have an Italian connection.

Birkett fought in the First World War as a captain in the Royal Field Artillery where his courage in action was underlined by no fewer than 18 mentions in dispatches and the award of the order of the Crown of Italy, Fifth Class (Knight).

The Order had been established by King Victor Emmanuel II in 1868 to commemorate the Unification of Italy and was awarded for civilian and military merit. But it is for his rugby exploits for which Birkett is deservedly inducted onto the World Rugby Museum's Wall of Fame.

He was a member of the England side that won the Championship in 1910 – the year that Twickenham was opened – and they opened in style beating Wales for the first time since 1898, scoring from the kick-off in a sensational start to the match and the season.

In all Birkett, who died in 1968 aged 83, scored ten tries and a drop goal for his country. His try scoring ratio per matches played as good as many of the modern day strike players. But Birkett's points tally of 34 is left in the shadows when compared with his co-inductee.

Diego Dominguez amassed a towering 983 points in his 74 appearances for Italy, placing him behind Wales Neil Jenkins (1,049), although the former fly-half insisted that he had actually passed the four-figure mark in his playing career.

"Don't forget I played two games for Argentina," he pointed out. "And I scored 27 points for them as well, so I actually have 1,010 points."

Dominguez remains one of Italy's most capped players his total of 74 keeping him in illustrious company, with the likes of his erstwhile partner at halfback Alessandro Troncon (101), and former lock Carlo Checchinato (83) among a handful of players ahead of him.

It was his sixth appearance for his adopted country (his mother is Italian) which Dominguez

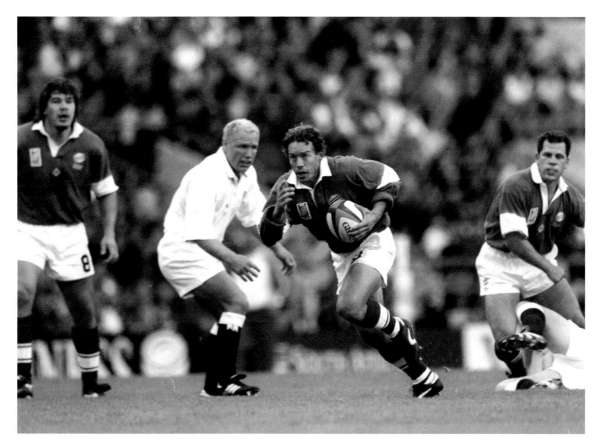

Potent points scorer... Italy fly-half Diego Dominguez

rated as one of his most memorable. It was his first appearance at Twickenham and it was in the second Rugby World Cup in 1991, the opponents were England.

"It was one of the best matches I have played in," recalled Dominguez, "and it was in the most famous Rugby stadium in the world.

"We had some very good players and a strong, aggressive pack. We had already beaten the United States and after the England defeat we gave the New Zealand All Blacks a good game at Leicester, losing by ten points.

"I had been to Twickenham before as a child and I have been since as a supporter of Italy. I watched the fantastic semi-final match in 1999 between France and New Zealand, which the French won. But it is the dream of every rugby player to play there and a bonus to score on the ground and I will keep the memory of that first appearance at Twickenham all my life."

The usually prolific Dominguez did manage to score on that first appearance, although his points tally was modest compared with his scoring feats during the rest of his distinguished career, he was restricted to a solitary conversion as Italy lost a tense match 36-6.

It wasn't much better; in fact Italy did a lot worse, eight years later when the two countries once again found themselves in the same group. The Azzurri found themselves on the end of a right old thrashing, losing 67-7. On this occasion though Dominguez scored all their points with a try and a conversion.

In between Dominguez converted all three of Italy's tries in an autumn international that they lost 54-21 to the host nation.

Dominguez insisted that Italy can only improve. Admission to the Six Nations was the single most critical feature of Italy's progress in the Rugby world.

"For me it was the most important moment in Italian Rugby history," said Dominguez, who, at the time of his interview, was based in France, but ran a sports-orientated business simultaneously in Argentina, and which therefore entailed him spending half of every month in South America.

"Getting into such an historic competition, there are no words to describe the powerful feelings it engendered at the time in Italy.

"And now more and more people are watching Rugby in Italy. The Stadio Flaminio has been attracting bigger crowds year by year since Italy were admitted in 2000.

"There are more sponsors, more supporters. Italy is a big country with a population of 54 million, and a rich country. Rugby in Italy will keep growing." As will the legend of Dominguez, a man with a golden boot if ever there was one.

Wade Dooley

England Second row

Born: 2.10.1957
Caps: 55
Debut: v Romania 1985
Last app: v Ireland 1993

Viv Jenkins

Wales Fullback

Born: 2.11.1911
Died: 5.1.2004
Caps: 14
Debut: v England 1933
Last app: v England 1939

As the years pass so the distance covered by Wade Dooley when he scored his third and final try for England on a memorable March day in 1992 increases.

"It gets longer every time I tell the story," said Dooley, of the day he won his 50th cap against Wales and helped England seal a back-to-back Grand Slam.

But Dooley is too honourable a man to allow myth to distort fact. "What actually happened was that Rob Andrew, who never ordinarily passed back inside, for some reason on this occasion did. And for some reason I, who never came up in support, found myself taking his flicked pass. It shocked me. And then I was driven over the line."

For Dooley it remains a very special day, one that had begun with the Preston Grasshoppers second row being invited to lead the team out on to the pitch to mark his half century of appearances for his country.

"I set off up the tunnel not realising that the boys had stood back. I went out on to the pitch on my own. I looked back and saw them all and I was there in the middle with this huge crowd cheering. It was amazing."

And it was all witnessed by Dooley's, then pregnant, wife Sharon, who was in the RFU committee box, sitting alongside Terry Waite, the former Beirut hostage. Dooley bowed out the following year with an impressive 55 caps to his name.

When he won his first cap against Romania he was then, at 6ft 8in, one of the tallest players to represent England. That debut also made him the first member of Lancashire constabulary to be capped.

Twickenham holds other memories for Dooley, who had played Rugby League until he became a police cadet in 1975. One of the most notable was when the then Prime Minister John Major was ushered into the home dressing room after an England win and Dooley witnessed a naked Micky Skinner, towel in left hand rubbing his hair, right hand modestly covering himself, making his way towards the former Conservative leader.

"They shook hands," said a flabbergasted Dooley, who, at the time of the interview, had just

Policing the line-out… England second row forward Wade Dooley

over two years to serve in the police force before embarking on a career as a landscape designer. "John Major did not even hesitate when Skinner's right hand was offered."

He also remembered a tussle with a groundsman at headquarters when the 1988 Australians complained that the grass was too long. Geoff Cooke, the manager, had to contact Dudley Wood to request that an inch be shaved off, in the event the groundsman compromised at half an inch. And England beat that pack of Wallabies as well.

Dooley's co-inductee on to the Wall of Fame is former Wales fullback **Vivian Jenkins**. He was a double Blue in cricket and rugby at Oxford, and he won 14 caps with Wales between 1933 and 1939. He also played cricket for Glamorgan, before going on to become a distinguished journalist covering cricket and rugby, first for the News of the World then for the Sunday Times, finally editing Rothman's Rugby Yearbook.

He had them gasping on the terraces when he scored a try against Ireland from fullback. The first Welshman to do so. It was another 33 years before Keith Jarrett became the second fullback to touch down in an international.

There was another first for Jenkins before that though, on his debut in 1933 against England at Twickenham – a debut he shared with two other Glamorgan cricketers, Wilf Wooller and Maurice Turnbull – as a member of the Wales team which recorded its first victory on the old 'Cabbage Patch', a win for which they had waited 23 years, Jenkins landed a conversion which was given as over by the Welsh touch judge, but which was ruled wide by referee Tom Bell.

Frik Du Preez

South Africa Second row

Born: 28.11.1935
Caps: 38
Debut: v England 1961
Last app: v Australia 1971

Ron Jacobs

England Prop

Born: 28.10.1928
Died: 10.11.2002
Caps: 29
Debut: v Wales 1956
Last app: v Scotland 1964

L egendary South African second row forward Frik Du Preez and England's doughty prop Ron Jacobs were the archetypal players of the amateur days. They loved the game beyond all else.

Not even the oppressive shadow of Apartheid, which darkened the game during their careers, could snuff out the candle each man held for the noble sport of rugby union.

They both played in the test at Headquarters in 1961. A demonstration-free match that was also, according to contemporary reports, free of anything remotely resembling exciting and expansive rugby.

South Africa won the match 5-0. But as unmemorable as the game might have been for England and their fans, Du Preez certainly had every reason to remember it with fondness, it was his international debut.

"I am not afraid to admit it," said Du Preez recently, "when I learned that I had been selected for the team to play England at Twickenham, I did cry, out of pride and joy. It was my first test. I was a surprise selection, because I hadn't been playing for my Province when I was picked. I had played for the Combined Forces against New Zealand and I played myself into the squad in that match."

His first impressions of the stadium were indelible. Du Preez recalled: "For every rugby player to play at Twickenham is something special, especially, like me, when you are winning your first cap. I remember the match. We beat England 5-0.

"When I ran on to the pitch I remember thinking that the crowd was very close to the touchline, and that is what made the atmosphere there so great.

"At Ellis Park you are far from the pitch. But at Twickenham the crowd is almost on top of the players, that's why I could feel how disappointed they were when we were winning in 1961."

That proximity of the crowd had its disadvantages as well. In a most un-Twickenham-like manner Du Preez, a goal-kicker of some note, found himself being slow-handclapped when preparing to kick the odd penalty. One contemporary commentator suggested that the 6ft 2in Du Preez was completely put off with one attempt, and he did miss a couple of kicks in each

Indelible memories of Twickenham… Springbok lock Frik Du Preez

half, although his memory fails him as to exactly how many attempts at goal he had in the whole match.

"I don't think any home crowd is always nice to the visiting team," Du Preez explained, "but it is part of the game I think. That didn't bother me. I had two shots at goal which I missed, but when they slow hand-clapped it did not put me off, I was just concentrating. So I won't blame the crowd for missing those kicks. I can't remember whether I had any penalty attempts in the second half."

What mattered most to Du Preez was that he enjoyed success with one very important kick – his conversion of fellow back rower Doug Hopwood's try shortly before half-time.

"It was nice just to put over the conversion. For every rugby player to play at Twickenham is something special, but when, like me, you are winning your first cap and you contribute to the score then it is even more so."

In fact according to Du Preez, he could have made an even greater contribution to the Springbok cause. He was on the brink of scoring a try when his moment of glory was rudely extinguished by the England scrum-half Dickie Jeeps.

Du Preez explained: "The ball went out to the wing, I was playing on the flank, I received the ball but I was half asleep, otherwise I could have scored a try. The wing gave me the ball, but as I went over the goal-line Dickie Jeeps, the England scrum-half managed to slap the ball out of my hand. If he hadn't done that I would have scored. It would have made my debut even better."

It was still a pretty impressive start to an international career which spanned 11 years, in which time Du Preez, who ended up in the second row, won 38 caps.

He was to appear at Twickenham again eight years later, on the Springboks' troubled 1969-70 tour of the British Isles. The jet-lagged Boks had scarcely landed before they opened their campaign against Oxford University. This match had been switched from Iffley Road because the police felt they would be unable to guarantee the safety of spectators and players in view of the anti-Apartheid demonstrations that had been threatened.

So the University authorities and the Rugby Football Union decided to switch the fixture to Twickenham, a decision made at the last minute in the hope that it would disrupt the protestors' plans.

Unsurprisingly perhaps, Du Preez merely remembered losing the match 6-3. "In 1969-70 we did lose to Oxford University, but I can't remember that tour very well."

It was remarkable that the Dark Blues and the Tourists were able to complete the match given the presence in the ground of the spectators. Only the West Stand was opened up to the public and some of the more militant demonstrators were among these spectators.

There were scuffles with police – 400 constables were on duty that day at a cost of some £4,000 to the RFU – a couple of arrests, a pitch 'invasion' by two protestors at half time, but the main attempt to disrupt the game was the blowing of referees' whistles, to try to make it difficult or even impossible for match official Mike Titcomb's genuine article to be distinguishable from the general cacophony. Fortunately the players coped and the South African management did not try to use the bizarre playing conditions and various distracting activities as excuses for what was a shock defeat.

And the Tourists, including Du Preez, had a far happier time on their return to the ground a fortnight or so later when they beat London Counties 22-6, and he was spared the misery of the 11-8 defeat, the Springboks' first in the short history of fixtures between these two countries, against England just before Christmas.

But Du Preez was back in action on the ground when the South Africans played, and won handsomely, their swansong of the tour against the Barbarians at the end of January 1970.

His final match at Twickenham came just over a year later when Du Preez was invited to partner another legendary lock, All Black Colin Meads, in the second row of the RFU President's XV against England, who were awarding caps for this prestigious match in April 1971 as part of the RFU's Centenary celebrations. And once more Du Preez was on the winning side, the glittering All Stars who included such luminaries as Jo Maso (France), Dawie de Villiers (South Africa), and Meads' New Zealand colleagues Brian Lochore and Ian Kirkpatrick.

Du Preez has since visited Twickenham as a guest of the International Rugby Board, after being inducted into the world governing body's Hall of Fame, when it is realised that he was also named South Africa's Rugby Player of the Twentieth Century by that country's fans of the game, it is a wonder that any more accolades will mean anything to him. But Du Preez welcomed the World Rugby Museum's honour with great humility.

"I feel honoured to have been inducted on to the Wall of Fame. Rugby has a great tradition and I am just honoured to be a part of that tradition. This is a great honour."

Ron Jacobs would almost certainly have endorsed such sentiments. The former prop, who played for Peterborough, Northampton and England, certainly made his mark on the game in this country, captaining England before going onto become president of the RFU in 1983.

Indeed he packed down against the selfsame South Africans who won that match at Twickenham in 1961 and in all he won 29 caps, captaining England in his final two appearances against France and Scotland in 1964. His record was impressive, in all those appearances Jacobs, nicknamed The Badger because of his formidable scrummaging technique, was only on the losing side ten times.

He was an inordinately strong man, in part due to the fact that he was a farmer, at Thorney near Peterborough. He stood 5ft 9in and weighed more than 15st – he was once described as being "... square-rigged and as broad as he is long." His powerful, but low slung stature coupled with his physique, meant he could get down lower than the majority of his opponents and, applying his strength give them a torrid time at the set piece.

Jacobs was a member of the first England team to win a post war Grand Slam, in 1957, part of an imposing front row comprising hooker and captain Eric Evans and George Hastings.

His term of office as RFU President coincided with the decision to send England on the controversial tour to South Africa in 1984. He was among a number of senior figures at Twickenham in favour of it, arguing that "...contact is more profitable and constructive than leaving South Africa out in the cold."

Jacobs went with the players as tour manager and off-field the trip went without a diplomatic hitch, unfortunately on the pitch England lost both tests, the last time the two countries were to play each other for eight years.

While Ron Jacobs will never be forgotten in his native East Midlands, he made 470 appearances for Northampton, the World Rugby Museum has now ensured that this stalwart of English rugby, together with South African legend Frik Du Preez, will forever be remembered on Twickenham's Wall of Fame.

David Duckham

England Wing

Born: 28.6.1946
Caps: 36
Debut: v Ireland 1969
Last app: v Scotland 1976

Serge Blanco

France Fullback

Born: 31.8.1958
Caps: 93
Debut: v South Africa 1980
Last app: v England 1991

D avid Duckham used to run rings around and through defensive walls, but there is one barrier he cannot avoid – the World Rugby Museum's Wall of Fame at Twickenham. The one-time golden boy of English rugby is fully deserving of the accolade as well, if only for his magnificent match against France in 1973.

Having played in two of England's heaviest defeats against the French in Paris in 1970 (13-35) and 1972 (12-37). Duckham said: "Playing in Paris was always a great experience, what with the volatility of the crowd, something which I found quite inspiring actually, and the various spectators' bands blaring away not to mention the live cockerels fluttering about the place.

"And we were outrun in both those games by the sheer pace of the French, although we did at least score some points in both games. There was something exhilarating about playing against them, even when we did get hammered. My goodness they were a class above us.

"Their dexterity was phenomenal, and we also underestimated their defensive qualities. In those days we used to think of the French as being weak in defence, but of course that was nonsense, they were just as strong as any other nation, but they used to capitalise on opposition errors and counter attack, just like New Zealand.

"They were always a different kettle of fish playing in Paris. They were a much better side at home in those days, in fact the nearest I got to a win in Paris was in 1974 when we drew 12-12.

"But at Twickenham the contrast was huge. Their attitude was certainly different when they came to us. We never saw them as a threat at Twickenham strangely."

In 1973 all the threat came from England, specifically from the left wing, one David Duckham, who scored two tries in England's 14-6 victory. He was unable to call to mind the first try in the opening half, but he had no trouble at all in going over for the second one.

"I remember the second try, because I had two Coventry players with me, Peter Preece and Geoff Evans and they were two players – and I am not saying this just because they were clubmates of mine – who had the pace to make a clean outside break.

"I remember Peter suddenly accelerated outside his opposite number, Claude Dourthe, with blistering pace – I had a hell of a job keeping up with him – and he rounded him completely,

A balanced, graceful and gifted runner... England golden boy David Duckham

and inevitably that created a two to one on the fullback. Peter just flicked the ball across to me and all I had to do was stay on my feet and fall over the line."

Duckham was a balanced runner, graceful on the ball and possessed of a devastating step off either foot, but he reckons that had he known then what he knows now about fitness and upper body strength he might have worked a little on that and he said: "I think I could have been yards quicker."

But Duckham was fast enough to run in ten tries in his 36 appearances for England between 1969 and 1976. And when he bowed out at the top, he took away with him some fond memories of Twickenham. "The atmosphere in the old stadium was very special and actually I am very sad that the modern stadium, I feel, is not the stadium it was.

"I am always going to be accused of being an old fogey and not being up-to-date, but I think Twickenham has lost some of its atmosphere.

"The angle of the cantilevers is so shallow that the seats in the back of the upper tiers are not only very high above the ground, but also so remote from the playing surface that the spectators up there must feel more detached from what is going on down on the field than they ever did before.

A true master of his art… the immensely talented Serge Blanco

"I think nowadays supporters really have to make a lot more noise to make an impact and re-create that old atmosphere. In my day if one supporter sneezed you could hear it anywhere around the ground. But not these days. Mind you in the 60s and 70s crowds were a lot less noisy."

At least today's crowds can cheer Duckham as loudly as they like as they view his name on the World Rugby Museum's Wall of Fame.

As for Duckham's co-inductee onto the Wall of Fame, **Serge Blanco**, he, and every one of his team-mates involved in possibly THE try of what was then just The Five Nations Championship, acquired legendary status back in March 1991, fittingly during what was the France fullback's final Championship match of his career.

Blanco had dazzled as a running, thinking fullback throughout his long and distinguished career. He counter-attacked with derring-do; he had pace; a swerve and a pass. And he was a lethal finisher, witness his 38 tries for France at almost one touchdown every two matches.

According to some pundits at the time the opening try of his final match, which was scored by France left winger Philippe Saint André, was the greatest try in the history of international rugby – presumably the Barbarians effort in 1973 does not fall into the full international category. It was certainly the most wonderful try scored at Twickenham in an international, that's for sure.

It started fairly innocuously. England had taken the lead in the second minute through the first of fullback Simon Hodgkinson's four penalty goals.

In the 13th minute he lined up another, but unfortunately pushed it to the right and France scrum-half Pierre Berbizier gathered the ball behind his line.

He hung on to the ball for a couple of seconds presumably debating the merit of touching down for the drop-out, the England players had already half turned away anticipating that decision.

But Blanco came on a looping run behind Berbizier, called for the ball and France were off. First Jean-Baptiste Lafond, then Didier Cambérabéro took the ball on down the right wing.

The ball was moved inside to Philippe Sella, who returned it to Cambérabéro. The fly-half chipped, re-gathered then put in a perfect cross kick to the middle of the field which Saint André, who had come scorching up, collected on the bounce before storming over the line to touch down under the posts and round off some 17 seconds of true Gallic flair.

But Blanco had not finished, he and Sella then conjured a magnificent try, almost as brilliant as that first one, for centre Franck Mesnel right at the death, which ensured that Rory Underwood's superb – and crucial – try on the half hour was well and truly overshadowed, even though it was the score that put England in charge and clinched for them the Grand Slam – the first of a memorable pair for Geoff Cooke and his squad.

Blanco is a man of few words when speaking of himself and his glittering career – he is somewhat more forthcoming when it comes to Rugby politics. All he would permit himself to say about the two tries was: "I remember the match and the tries as if it was yesterday.

"There are matches which stay with you for ever, and which send you off the pitch with an enormous sense of satisfaction, no matter what the result. This was one of those matches."

And Blanco has nothing but good things to say about Twickenham. "In those days it was one of those stadia which, thanks to the proximity of the spectators to the pitch, created a special atmosphere, unique to the place."

Given that Blanco's record at Twickenham during his 93-cap, 11-year career, boasted three wins and a draw in half a dozen visits, it is probably not surprising that he has fond memories of the place.

He recalled another French try at Twickenham which has stayed with him: "It was in 1987," said Blanco, "and on this occasion France won and Sella scored a try from an interception."

Sella anticipated a pass from England scrum-half Richard Hill to Rob Andrew, collected the ball, and then ran 65 metres for the telling score.

His strangest memory of the ground was playing for the Barbarians once against Harlequins and what struck Blanco was that there were only 7,000 spectators in the echoing stadium.

But Blanco's conclusion about Twickenham is: "It seems to me that all the matches played at Twickenham are memorable ones, whether they are won or lost; but this is something that can only be appreciated when one's playing career is over, then a player comes to understand that in playing at the ground he has played a very small part in the history of Rugby Union."

Now Blanco has been accorded a grander place in the history of the game, as an inductee on the Wall of Fame. "It is a signal honour and I am proud to have been considered for this by the English."

Xavier Dutour

France Fullback

Born:6.12.1886
Died:22.5.1978
Caps: 6
Debut: v England 1911
Last app: v Scotland 1913

Brian Moore

England Hooker

Born: 11.1.1962
Caps: 64
Debut: v Scotland 1987
Last app: v France 1995

Xavier Dutour, who is revered as one of the pioneers of what the French term 'noble sport' and which would translate as sportsmanship, made a little piece of history when he was inducted on to Twickenham's World Rugby Museum's Wall of Fame.

One of Dutour's distinctions, among many, was that he was a member of the France team which first played at Twickenham in 1911.

It was only England's third test at the ground – the first two having been played there in the previous season against Wales and Ireland.

It also marked Dutour's international debut, although sadly it was not the stuff of which dreams are made, since France lost by what remains their biggest losing margin to date – 37-0, although the most points they have conceded was at the same venue 90 years later in 2001 – but at least by wearing the No15 shirt in a side captained by the legendary Marcel Communeau he had shared in another piece of rugby history.

Dutour played for Stade Toulousain while winning his half dozen caps, becoming, incidentally, the first native of the Auvergne to represent his country. He had earlier been involved in the founding of Clermont-Ferrand's first civilian rugby team known as La Sportive in 1904.

He then went off to play in the colours of the Club Amicale Sportif de Grand Air, where he stayed for a season or two before enrolling at the veterinary college in Toulouse in 1907. While there he shared in the club's Championship-winning year in 1912 following a narrow victory over Racing Club de France.

After tasting defeat in all six of his appearances for his country he quit Stade Toulousain in 1913, returning to the Auvergne where he turned out for AS Michelin until the First World War intervened.

As first, a veterinary officer then later a captain in the French Artillery, he was awarded the Croix de Guerre and had a further three citations for his bravery in the field. Later, in peacetime, he was appointed Chevalier de la Legion d'Honneur in 1936.

He attempted to start up another rugby club in Lezoux, the village where he finally settled,

The scourge of France... Brian Moore, 'The Pitbull', England's ferocious hooker

not far from his home town of Moissat in the Puy-de-Dome. In addition to his veterinary practice he was also elected on to the local council, which he served for a staggering 46 years, serving as deputy mayor for a quarter of a century during that time.

He was the founding president of the association for Auvergne French internationals and died, aged 92 in April 1978.

He is joined on the Wall of Fame by Brian Moore, England's second most capped hooker, having ceded first place to Steve Thompson during the 2011 Six Nations Championship. Moore's 64 international appearances embraced no fewer than 10 confrontations with the French, the final one being in his last match in the 1995 Rugby World Cup in South Africa.

Moore was nicknamed 'The Pitbull' because of his dogged, ferocious approach to his play; nothing illustrates that better than the way he used to make a point of getting into the faces of the French, knowing that if they lost their temper, they would inevitably lose control of the game and they frequently did, most famously in Paris in 1992 when England were well along the path to winning their second Grand Slam.

Moore enjoyed a staggeringly successful record against France throughout his career. 'The Pitbull' tasted defeat in his first and last appearances against Les Bleus, while in between he shared in eight victories over France.

Moore also participated in all three of England's Grand Slam successes in the 1990s, retiring after England's final match of the 1995 Rugby World Cup, the third place play-off at Loftus Versfeld, Pretoria; that was also the year of England's third Slam.

Francois Pienaar

South Africa Wing forward

Born: 2.1.1967
Caps: 29
Debut: v France 1993
Last app: v New Zealand 1996

Norman Wodehouse

England Forward

Born: 18.5. 1887
Died: 4.7.1941
Caps: 14
Debut: v France 1910
Last app: v Scotland 1913

Twickenham holds a special place in **Francois Pienaar's** memory and that is some achievement given that this is the man who, as captain of South Africa, was the centre of one of the sport's most emotional moments when he lifted the World Cup at Ellis Park in 1995 and consigned to dim memory the years of sporting isolation.

"Twickenham is very special to me," revealed Pienaar "Because I played in the Saracens team which won the first trophy in the club's history, when we beat Wasps in the Tetley's Bitter Cup final. After the World Cup in 1995 that 48-18 victory is one of the most memorable highlights of my career."

Pienaar's elevation to the Wall of Fame at Twickenham is another for his memories. "It is a great honour to be the first South African to be placed on the Wall of Fame", said the former Saracens chief executive. "Twickenham has always been special for me, even before I played there, because we were able to see the games broadcast during the years of isolation and there were some fantastic matches.

"And when I first went there in 1992, as a spectator during South Africa's first tour since coming back into the international fold (I did not make the squad that time). It was an amazing experience. I remember I was sitting in the West Stand and it was there I heard for the first time, 'Swing low, sweet chariot'. It gave me goose bumps."

Pienaar's next visit to headquarters was also memorable. It was 1995 and by then he was captain of the World Champions. "We were very motivated for that test against England," he remembered. "It was vitally important that we finished what had been an unforgettable year undefeated and on a high."

Twickenham did the Rainbow Warriors proud. It was a sell-out at its new capacity of 75,000. And South Africa beat England 24–14.

Pienaar was the second World Cup winning captain after Australia's Nick Farr-Jones to be inducted to the Wall of Fame, and he certainly had an impact at the ground, but so too did his fellow inductee, **Norman Wodehouse**. He was the first captain to lead his country to a Grand Slam, a feat England achieved in 1913, the year before the Great War began.

Crowning glory... South Africa captain Francois Pienaar with the 1995 World Cup

Wodehouse had already shared England's Championship triumph of 1910 and he went on to captain his country in six matches, including the whole of that successful inaugural Grand Slam season. The outbreak of the First World War brought a premature end to what would certainly have been an even more illustrious career.

While there is no doubting Wodehouse's courage on the pitch, be it for England, United Services, Portsmouth or for the Royal Navy, there is also no doubting his outstanding bravery when serving his country in both World Wars.

It was as a gunnery officer taking part in the Battle of Jutland, chiefly on the battleship HMS Revenge, that Wodehouse dived into the ice cold waters to save a seaman who had fallen overboard from another vessel. For his selfless act of bravery Wodehouse was awarded the Royal Humane Society Silver Medal. By the time he retired from the Royal Navy in 1940 Wodehouse had reached the rank of Vice-Admiral.

But, typical of the man, he did not remain in retirement for long, re-enlisting, as did so many officers, and returning as Commodore (Second Class) Royal Naval Volunteer Reserve.

He was assigned to escorting and protecting merchant navy vessels, which at that time were the prey of the so-called 'wolves of the sea' the dreaded German Untersee, or U-Boats, and in July 1941 Wodehouse's ship the Robert L Holt met the U69 and was sunk by gunfire. There were no survivors.

W.J.A. Davies

England Outside half

Born: 21.6.1890
Died: 26.4.1967
Caps: 22
Debut: v South Africa 1913
Last app: v France 1923

Gareth Edwards

Wales Scrum-half

Born: 12.7.1947
Caps: 53
Debut: v France 1967
Last app: v France 1978

It has been one of Rugby's enduring mysteries of the Post War era, albeit perhaps not quite one of the most intriguing, nevertheless it has finally been solved. It took place on a one-time Cabbage Patch, but there was no need of a Miss Marple, Hercule Poirot or Sherlock Holmes to solve this particular 30-year-old whodunnit, merely the confession of the guilty party.

It was at Twickenham in 1970, England were leading Wales and half-time was just seconds away. A ruck formed and a tide of red shirts flowed over and through everything and everybody who was in their way, including the French referee Robert Calmet.

When it was over and play had moved on, M. Calmet remained on the ground clutching a broken left leg. Subsequent records of the game, in respected books and annuals, merely mention that M. Calmet had been in a collision with an unnamed player.

Finally that player's identity can be revealed. It was Wales captain, **Gareth Edwards**. "It was a memorable match but for the wrong reasons," recalled Edwards. "I made a break and I ran over the referee. I remember turning around afterwards and seeing him on the ground with what turned out to be a broken leg and Johnny Johnson came on as his replacement.

"Then I got injured midway through the second half and had to go off. My replacement was Chico Hopkins, from Maesteg RFC, and he immediately set up JPR Williams for a try before scoring the fourth himself, then setting up Barry John for the drop goal which ensured victory."

Edwards, having made his debut aged 19, went on to become the youngest player ever to captain Wales, when he was appointed to lead them against Scotland in 1968 when he was 20. In all he captained Wales on 13 occasions.

Remarkably all 53 of his caps for Wales were won consecutively and dotted among them are the 20 tries the former Millfield School pupil scored for his country.

England's rugby headquarters holds other great memories for Edwards. "On my very first appearance there, and my fourth for Wales, two years earlier, I scored my first international try in the 11 – 11 draw."

There then followed a stream of unforgettable visits until, a decade after that first try, came

The scrum-halves' scrum-half... Wales' brilliant Gareth Edwards

one of the most moving moments of Edwards' distinguished career. "It was February 1978 and I was winning my 50th cap. The captain, Phil Bennett, asked me to lead the team out.

"As I emerged from the tunnel, I was greeted by cheers and applause from the whole crowd, English and Welsh fans alike. It was very emotional. I ran onto the pitch, then turned, as I always did, looking for a team-mate to whom I could pass the ball, but of course there was no one there, Ray Gravell was holding them all back in the tunnel to let me enjoy those few special moments.

"But it was not over, because later, at the post-match dinner, I was presented with a rose bowl by the RFU. They had had fifty made to mark their centenary and I was presented with No 50. It was a most generous and thoughtful gift." Now Edwards has received a further, and most deserving award from the RFU.

He is joined on the Wall of Fame by another Welshman **W J A 'Dave' Davies**, who was born in Pembroke in 1890, but who chose to play his rugby over the border and led England to the Grand Slam in 1921 and 1923.

For something like 66 years Davies was England's most capped fly-half with 22 appearances until Rob Andrew's emergence towards the end of the 20th century, the Wasps outside half passing the mark in 1989. Davies captained his country on 11 occasions, but his career was interrupted by the First World War.

Then, as a naval officer, Davies served aboard HMS Iron Duke, then HMS Queen Elizabeth and was appointed OBE in 1919 in recognition of his naval duty.

Rather like Edwards, Davies was something of an all-round athlete, winning the Champions Cup as best athlete of the year while at Greenwich. The only time Davies experienced defeat in an England jersey was on his debut against South Africa in 1913, when England were beaten 9-3 by South Africa. The remainder of his career, which fell either side of the First World War, saw him on the winning side in all 21 Five Nations matches in which he played.

Coincidentally Davies died on April 26th 1967, just 25 days after Edwards made his debut for Wales.

Eric Evans
England Hooker

Born: 1.2.1921
Died: 12.1.1991
Caps: 30
Debut: v Australia 1948
Last app: v Scotland 1958

Gavin Hastings
Scotland Fullback

Born: 3.1.1962
Caps: 61
Debut: v France 1986
Last app: v New Zealand 1995

Even in those pre-pro days the players were pampered. Cambridge, barely out of Pampers as rugby players, were no exception; in fact', as befits one of the country's pillars of the rugby establishment, the Light Blues had a physiotherapist.

And not just any physiotherapist, either. No this was a physio with a difference. A basic difference. And the Jobsworth at the entrance to the dressing rooms was not going to let her in, to mix with all those male athletes to strut their stuff at HQ. No, not under any circumstances, not over his dead body.

The Cambridge captain was **Gavin Hastings** and he takes up the story. "It was 1985, said the former Lions and Scotland captain. "I was captain of Cambridge.

"We got off the coach and all the boys marched into the changing rooms, but this doddery old man said, 'No women in here', when our physio went to follow us in.

"We had to send one of our officials into the smoke-filled committee rooms above us to persuade a Twickenham bigwig to overrule the steward. I think this was the very first time a woman had been to Twickenham. In fact I think she may have been one of the first female physios in the country."

It was not Hastings's first visit to HQ. His first was with the Light Blues the year before, a match which they won comfortably. Under his leadership 12 months later an exciting game ended in defeat by one point and thereafter Twickenham was an unhappy place for Hastings.

"That first Varsity match was a great thrill for me," said Hastings, who retired from the game without a backward glance, after the 1995 Rugby World Cup, having amassed a total of 733 points with the Lions and Scotland.

"There were present and future internationals playing, Rob Andrew, Fran Clough, Mark Bailey, Kevin Simms and we won 32-6. But whenever I went to Twickenham with Scotland it was not such a productive place."

Four of Hastings' 56 Scotland caps were earned at Twickenham and he explained: "We always seemed to play second fiddle to England in those days. Twickenham was a very difficult place for visiting sides, especially before the reconstruction.

Biting team-talk... England hooker Eric Evans, the great motivator

The complete fullback... Scotland's much-capped Gavin Hastings

"There was a fantastic atmosphere, the old stands were so much closer to the pitch, the crowd were almost on top of you. These days it is a little more remote, although England have taken to it."

It was the scene of the last Five Nations (as it then was) appearance, and for the fourth time in his career Scotland scored 12 points, and for the fourth time it was nowhere near enough.

Finally Hastings has become a winner at Twickenham. He has been inducted onto the Wall of Fame. "I am delighted and very honoured," said Hastings. "I think it is quite something when you are recognised outside your own country; it underlines the universality of rugby."

He is joined in the Wall of Fame by the late **Eric Evans**, the hooker who captained England to the 1957 Grand Slam, the last leg of which was against Scotland at Twickenham. One of Evans' former England and Barbarians team-mates, Chris Winn, the wing, once observed that when Evans was giving a team talk he was barely comprehensible because he gave the stirring speech without his teeth. But that season under Evans guidance the England side certainly had some bite.

Evans played for Sale and Lancashire as well as for his country, and when he was appointed to captain England for the first time in the Five Nations match against Wales at Twickenham on January 21 1956, it was 11 days short of his 35th birthday, making him the oldest player to lead the red rose team.

Barry John
Wales Outside half

Gerald Davies
Wales Wing

Born: 6.1.1945
Caps: 25
Debut: v Australia 1966
Last app: v France 1972

Born: 7.2.1945
Caps: 46
Debut: v Australia 1966
Last app: v Australia 1978

There is an old joke in which four Welsh Rugby legends, in this case Mervyn Davies, Gareth Edwards, **Barry John** and **Gerald Davies** stand on the banks of the River Taff in Cardiff, a stone's throw from the Arms Park as was, and nowadays the Millennium Stadium.

"Let's cross over the river here," said Gerald. And the lightning fast winger, whose electric pace and beautifully balanced running left so many defenders for dead throughout his distinguished career, races lightly across the river. John follows, his feet seeming barely to touch the surface.

"On my way," said Gareth, and the greatest Wales scrum-half ever joins Gerald and Barry on the opposite bank. Mervyn goes to follow them and instantly plunges up to his waist in the chilling waters.

His three Wales colleagues start to laugh at the floundering forward. "He obviously didn't know about the stepping stones," said Gareth.

"What stepping stones?" asked Gerald and Barry ….

Over the years that joke has been adapted to depict pretty well every great Wales player as the God-like figure who can walk upon water.

But there is no doubt that Gerald Davies and his fellow inductee Barry John on the World Rugby Museum's Wall of Fame at Twickenham did appear to be capable of near miraculous feats at the height of their pomp when Wales ruled the Five Nations Championship throughout the 1970s.

John, who scored 90 points in 25 appearances for Wales, was the silkiest and most elusive of runners, perfectly balanced and possessed of some kind of foresight which allowed him to see where a gap was about to appear in a defensive line so he could ghost through before any of the mere mortals who comprised the opposition, was aware of the chink.

He could also kick off either foot and his superb footballing brain enabled him to use feet and head for some of the most devilish of tactical kicks, and that was with a leather ball, which was not coated in a plastic laminate to render it waterproof, but rather it would soak up moisture and grow heavier and less aerodynamic as the game wore on, yet still John produced

King John I of Wales... the legendary fly-half Barry John in his pomp

masterful kicks that repeatedly turned opponents back and set up Wales in superb attacking positions.

John never played on a losing Wales team against England at Twickenham. In 1968 his drop goal helped ensure Wales escaped with an 11-11 draw.

Two years later he scored a try and landed another drop goal at Headquarters as Wales emerged 17-13 victors and on his last appearance there John kicked a conversion and two penalties in a 12-3 victory.

Barry John was dubbed 'King' and is still worshipped, quite rightly, throughout the Principality.

But Davies is equally treasured by the Welsh Nation. He began his international career in the centre, but by the time of his retirement from the international stage in 1978 he had built up a reputation as one of the most lethal wings in the 20th century game.

Yet despite the fact that he scored 20 tries in just 46 international appearances for Wales,

Wales wing Gerald Davies, revelled in the brooding Twickenham atmosphere

there is one glaring omission in Davies' impressive rugby CV – the former Cardiff and London Welsh threequarter never scored a try in five visits with Wales to Twickenham.

It is not something that Davies dwelled on though. He was quite sanguine, indeed almost contrary about it. "Although wings are finishers I actually preferred to create tries.

"Sometimes when you were on the wing all you had to do was run it in after your teammates had done all the hard work. I liked the idea of being the creator."

Davies, who made five appearances for the British Isles and Irish Lions in 1968 and 1971, saw fun in the centre's role as he would try to create something out of nothing.

"There is a sense of mischief in using your skills to outwit the opposition." He certainly did that throughout his career.

And although Davies did not score a try in internationals at Twickenham the stadium has a special place in his heart.

"The old Twickenham was an atmospheric setting, no doubt about that. As you stepped out of the tunnel on to the pitch. In those days the fixture list was fixed. Wales always opened their Five Nations campaign against England in January.

"So this meant that every other year we would go to Twickenham in mid-winter and it always seemed to be a dark, forbidding place. That had nothing to do with the crowd, it was simply because of the way that the stands were constructed. They cast a shadow over the pitch. There was a sense that it was hanging over you. I can never remember playing an international in sunshine, it was always under a louring sky, with dark brooding clouds.

"But Twickenham was known in those days as the Cathedral of Rugby, and for all its forbidding nature in January, whenever I went there for the Middlesex Sevens, which traditionally brought the curtain down on the season in May, the contrast could not have been greater.

"Then, in bright sunshine and with the intimacy of the packed stands, it was an exciting place to be. It was a real festival of rugby, and I scored plenty of tries there then.

"In the 50s and 60s Twickenham was not the 'Away Day' trip that the motorways have turned it into. For players and supporters alike it was a weekend break. And every Welshman going to the match seemed to stay in the Regent's Palace Hotel in the West End of London.

"I seem to remember that supporters used to get on to the pitch before a game and on one occasion in the late 50s Terry Davies, the Wales fullback, was unable to kick at goal because the crossbars had gone missing."

Twickenham was also special because of the fixture against England, and while Davies insisted that any animosity between the two sides was a figment of media imagination, nevertheless he acknowledged that every match, home and away, against Red Rose teams was not easy.

"They were always tough games at Twickenham, and although we won a couple of times up there, I don't think we ever entered a match against England on their home ground as favourites.

"For a start," and you could almost see him shudder at the memory, "England always seemed to have big beefy forwards, and, to a man, they were intensely competitive."

In case anyone thinks that Davies never scored against England, he did, indeed famously, on one occasion, he scored two touchdowns against England – unfortunately that feat at Cardiff in 1967 was overshadowed, not by any hulking stands, but rather by a Newport schoolboy, Keith Jarrett, who scored 19 points for Wales that same day.

It was just as well that the World Rugby Museum chose to remember Davies in this way as he and Barry 'King' John, joined an élite band of international players from all over the Rugby world on the Wall of Fame, a Pantheon of outstanding talents who have given so much pleasure to so many at Twickenham over the years.

Gordon Brown

Scotland Second row

Born: 1.11.1947
Died: 19.3.2001
Caps: 30
Debut: v South Africa 1969
Last app: v Ireland 1976

Ian Smith

Scotland Wing

Born: 31.10.1903
Died: 18.9.1972
Caps: 32
Debut: v Wales 1924
Last app: v Ireland 1933

It is a gross injustice that **Gordon Brown** is not around to celebrate his induction on to the Twickenham Wall of Fame, there can be few more worthy candidates for the signal honour. Sadly, Broon frae Troon died in 2000, otherwise he would have enjoyed replaying his memories of playing at Twickenham.

He certainly has reason to remember his first visit to Billy Williams 'Cabbage Patch'. That was back in 1971, when Scotland descended on a ground where they had not won a match since Wilson Shaw's 1938 team had picked off the auld enemy.

The Brown family had come down in force too. In addition to Gordon, there was older brother Peter, while father Jock was the Scotland physio.

Brown was in the second row pitted against Nigel Horton, no mean opponent and someone who was unafraid of the odd bit of extra-curricular activity off the ball. And that was another reason why Brown was to remember the game with such clarity.

There was an inevitable confrontation early on, Brown described the incident in his autobiography Broon from Troon.

He described how he and Big Nigel had a set-to, and for a change it was Horton who needed the restorative properties of the magic sponge. The trouble was, Brown explained, that the English sponge was already being used on John Pullin, the hooker.

The solution to the mini dilemma was for Brown's father Jock to come on the field and mop up the damage that his son had inflicted on the burly England lock. Brown added that Big Nigel was not amused.

When brother Peter Brown, who had scored one of Scotland's three tries then converted Chris Rea's last minute touchdown to secure victory for Scotland, Horton was even less amused. He refused to shake hands with Gordon Brown and was reported as saying, "I'll see you next week."

That was a reference to the centenary international between England and Scotland at Murrayfield the following Saturday, but Horton was dropped for that match. However, the same Scotland team that had triumphed at Twickenham, won the Centenary clash in convincing style.

Brown shares his honour with another legendary Scottish international **Ian Smith**, dubbed the 'Flying Scot' and one of the most potent of try scorers in an era, the 1920s and 1930s, when tries were at a premium.

He was possessed of scorching pace and reports at the time claim he was a match for a contemporary of his, Eric Liddell.

He was actually born in Melbourne and brought up in New Zealand, but he was educated at Winchester and qualified to play for Scotland through his lineage in the Borders.

Smith's first visit to Twickenham coincided with the victory over England on March 21 1925 that clinched the first of Scotland's (to date) three Grand Slams. Oddly Smith, who was the world's leading try scorer from 1932 until 1987 when Australia's David Campese passed his mark of 24 tries, failed to score in that match. Astonishingly, Smith remains Scotland's leading try-scorer some 77 years after his retirement, sharing the honour with another wing, Tony Stanger, although his claim to have scored most tries (24) in the Five/Six Nations Championship in his career was finally overtaken by Ireland's Brian O'Driscoll in the 2011 Six Nations Championship.

That was clearly a glitch though, because he subsequently went on to score two tries in four further Calcutta Cup matches, although he only achieved the feat of a try double at Twickenham on one occasion, in 1926. Towards the end of his illustrious career Smith stung England for a solitary try at Twickenham in 1932, the year of his penultimate Calcutta Cup match against the 'auld enemy'.

He ran in four tries against France in 1925, and repeated the feat in the same season against Wales, having crossed the Welsh line three times on his international debut the season before.

He wrapped up his playing career in some style, captaining Scotland to the Triple Crown in 1933.

Richard Hill

England Wing forward

Born: 23.5.1973
Caps: 71
Debut: v Scotland 1997
Last app: v Australia 2004

Jonah Lomu

New Zealand Wing

Born: 12.5.1975
Caps: 63
Debut: v France 1994
Last app: v Wales 2002

The World Rugby Museum's Wall of Fame features giants of the game and this pair most certainly fall into that category – one them literally. **Jonah Lomu** was a massive presence on the rugby field.

In the case of **Richard Hill**, had not injury cruelly ended his career, then he would almost certainly have come close to a century of appearances for England.

Nevertheless, the former Saracens flanker still did enough to more than deserve his status as one of the legendary figures in the world game, let alone in his home country.

As for New Zealand winger Lomu, his career was blighted by illness and injury otherwise he would also have added to the 63 appearances he made for the Land of the Long White Cloud.

When he first came on the scene Lomu's 6ft 5in 18½st frame sent tremors through pitches and opponents alike.

He might only have been aged 19 years and 45 days – making him to this day, the youngest player to make his debut for the All Blacks – but he still looked unstoppable, and frequently was. Just ask Tony Underwood, the former England wing, or indeed any member of the Red Rose team that was smashed aside in the 1995 Rugby World Cup when Lomu ran in four tries. He went on to score a staggering 37 tries for his country, putting him right up there with the best of the best.

But Lomu was possessed of more than mere physical presence, as Hill, who came up against him once or twice in his 71-cap career, said: "Jonah Lomu knew when to use his power and when to use his pace. That was the phenomenon of Jonah when he came along. It wasn't just a case of him being a battering ram, he did have a good sidestep, and the ability, once he was through the hole, actually to accelerate away.

"When he came on to the scene he was a class of player that hadn't been seen before. It was almost creating a mould for others coming` in behind him."

As for stopping this behemoth of a wing threequarter, who boasted a 10.8 second 100 metres, Hill has some eminently sensible advice for would-be tacklers of Lomu. "Certainly, from having played against him, I know you don't ever want to let him get up a head of steam.

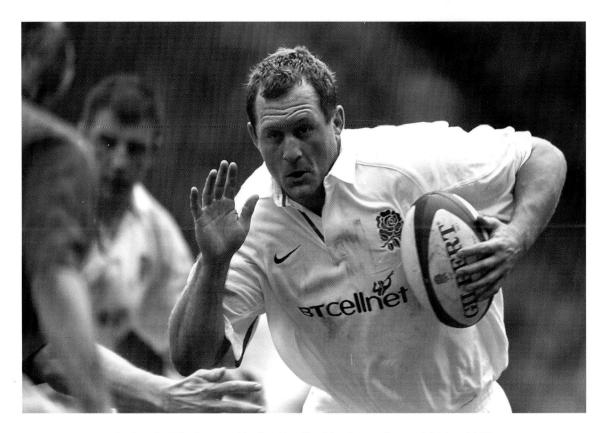

An irresistible force... England's gifted back row forward Richard Hill

"That was one of the key things when tackling him, taking the man and the ball. Actually start tackling him while he is concentrating on catching the ball. He was difficult to stop once he had got going, and when he did it was better to tackle him from behind, not from in front."

In December 1997 England took on the whole All Blacks team head-on in an epic match, described by observers at the time as "stupendous" a game where the rugby was "played at a stupefying pace and with a ferocious intensity sustained from beginning to end."

It was one of two matches between England and New Zealand at Twickenham which Hill remembered with pride, the second one was in 2002. But for Hill the first of those tests was the more important.

"I think the first one probably had a significance, when we drew 26-26 in 1997. Firstly because of the first half performance that we put in. We scored three tries in the first half, playing a very good brand of rugby.

"But I think the match also probably opened our eyes to the fact that, although we had great ability, we didn't have the fitness to back it up, and that lack of fitness allowed New Zealand to come back in. We had to come back with a penalty right at the end to draw it."

Hill had personal cause to recall the historic draw, because he scored one of those first half tries – he was to go on to score a total of 12 for England – and not content with touching the

England's nemesis... New Zealand's giant threequarter Jonah Lomu

ball down once, Hill touched it down a second time to be sure, to be sure, as he explained: "I remember that Will Greenwood seemed to be doing a dancing run that looked as if it was never going to end.

"But I kept following him, kept supporting and eventually I think he threw the ball on to the floor at my feet and I managed to scoop it up and drop down. I remember putting it on the line, but having done so, one of the New Zealand defenders managed to tackle me and knocked me back infield, so I went back to try to score it again, just to make sure, if there was any doubt first time. There was no grandiose solo run or anything like that on my part, just some support play for Will."

It was an important score and a major contribution to the team ethic, and the result was also to have a long term influence on the England team. "After that draw we knew we could stay in there, although we knew we did have some work to do. But there was a belief that we could actually do it now."

Fast forward five years and there was proof that England had learned the lessons of that thrilling confrontation with the All Blacks when the two sides met once more at Twickenham, because they did not stop at a draw, this time they went on to record a victory over the All Blacks, at that time only England's fourth in 14 Tests against these opponents at Headquarters. True they came close to snatching defeat from the jaws of victory after throwing away a lead of 31-14 with three quarters of the match gone, but this time they had the fitness and the self-belief to hold on.

Early in the 21st Century England were on something of a roll, performing clinically and well under Clive Woodward and as Hill recalled: "In 2002 we were starting to build on that confidence on the way to the 2003 World Cup. We knew that these were the sides we needed to beat, and here we were actually rewarded with a victory against New Zealand."

In addition to their superlative organisation and approach under Woodward, there was also another factor to be taken into consideration when England beat the All Blacks in 2002 – the venue.

Twickenham is a special place and no one knows that better than Hill. "Your home venue is a massive environment for you," he said. "An environment where you have to create a winning habit. We all know that playing at home actually means you expect to have a big following, therefore the atmosphere created by the support of the team is that much greater.

"Twickenham can be intimidating to opponents, without a doubt. As long as you are doing the business on the pitch, backed up by the supporters, then it can be difficult for the opposition. And you can then use that to your own advantage.

"And when you are going through particularly good runs, as we were fortunate enough to be doing at Twickenham at that time, the crowd continually gets behind you and there is an excitement and a buzz whenever some of the exciting players in our side got the ball in their hands.

"Whenever Jason Robinson caught the ball, it didn't matter whether he was 50 metres, 60 metres or 70 metres behind you, you knew, as a forward, that you were going to have to get back, that he was going to have a go, because everyone wanted to see him have a go. And that was why he was being picked. It was great to see. It was great that he had the confidence to do it."

That home advantage is true for all teams, as Hill admitted: "I have played in some fairly intimidating places around the world and you can end up surviving off scraps from the home team; when things aren't going well that is not such an easy option."

To listen to Hill though, Twickenham can have a pretty profound effect on a debutant there. "Everyone has memories of their first game. I'd experienced Twickenham as a spectator, I'd played a match there for my school, a couple of matches with my college, but never to a full house. I was very fortunate that my first international cap was at Twickenham, against Scotland in 1997

"I remember warming up and I thought 'This is OK'. But there had been maybe 10,000 spectators in the stadium when we had walked out to warm-up well before the kick-off.

"Later, to be in the changing room and to hear that noise building up outside, as kick-off drew nearer, it gave me goosebumps. The sound in the tunnel as we ran out was such a colossal noise, it was something I had never experienced before and certainly I know that it gave me a positive mental lift. It enthused me to want to get into the game and be all action but although I was doing my job I had to be a little bit careful and not get over-enthusiastic and make errors."

If it had not been for sports science, even now, Hill would have harboured warm memories of the changing rooms, and, inevitably, the famous individual baths, deep and long, and so inviting with their plumes of steam, after a bitterly cold 80 minutes on the pitch.

"There is no doubt that unless you had been in some luxurious place, the baths at Twickenham were amazing. But it got ruined the day the sports scientists decided you weren't allowed to have a bubble bath after an international, which is pretty much what we were allowed when I first played for England. Often we would be lying in the bath with a can of sponsored lager or something.

"Then they changed the rules and we could only have ice baths. They put a stop watch on you and you had to stay in it for five minutes. The day that all started was quite a bad day."
There are other special memories that Hill cherished as well. "When you started you had a wooden plaque with an English rose with your name on it that was put over your place in the changing room at Twickenham.

"The other thing I remember about playing at Twickenham was that internal warmth you derived from running out onto the pitch, I think that is probably the most special memory for me, just running out on the pitch and knowing everyone in the crowd is behind you."

Henceforth it will not just be the crowds of the past, but those of the future who will be behind Hill following his elevation on to the World Rugby Museum's Wall of Fame at Twickenham.

"It is a true honour. I am very honoured to be there. I thoroughly enjoyed my time in the game and I wouldn't change it for anything."

Spoken like a true giant of the game of rugby union, which Hill and Lomu most certainly are.

Colin Windon

Australia Wing forward

Born: 8.11.1921
Died: 3.11.03
Caps: 20
Debut: v New Zealand 1946
Last app: v New Zealand 1952

Jason Robinson

England Fullback

Born: 30.7.1974
Caps: 51
Debut: v Italy 2001
Last app: v South Africa 2007

Speed is a common factor with the latest two inductees to the World Rugby Museum's Wall of Fame at Twickenham. **Col Windon**, regarded as one of Australia's finest breakaway forwards was nicknamed 'Breeze', because he ran like the wind.

It has to be said that England's **Jason Robinson** probably ran faster than that, not for nothing was he dubbed 'Billy Whizz' after the speedy comic character.

In fact speed seems to have been a feature of Jason Robinson's rugby union career. He was certainly one of the fastest players to grace Twickenham and indeed rugby union.

But the speed was not confined to his running on the pitch. Robinson made his debut for Sale at the beginning of November 2000 and just three months later, on February 17, to be precise, he made his England debut. Fast tracking by anyone's standards, and appropriate given Robinson's natural speed.

On that memorable day Robinson, who was selected as a replacement, wasted little time in winning over the fans. He recalled: "My England debut against Italy was a massive day for me, there's no doubt about it. I hadn't been in Rugby Union very long before I got the call-up.

"It was bizarre because I can remember sitting on the bench and hearing people around me shouting 'Get him on, get him on'. It was great the way Twickenham took to me. It was just amazing. I hadn't even touched the ball, but the crowd was really looking forward to me getting the ball in my hands and seeing what I could do."

It was the start of what for many was an all-too brief career, albeit Robinson still notched up 51 caps for England between 2001 and 2007.

He retired from international rugby not once but twice, and speed features again here, because just 12 months into his second, and final, retirement Robinson has been inducted on to the World Rugby Museum's Wall of Fame, at Twickenham. The Wall was set to commemorate not just great England players, but greats from all over the rugby world since Twickenham first staged internationals on what was once affectionately known as Billy Williams' Cabbage Patch.

Robinson appreciated the signal honour that has been conferred upon him by the World Rugby Museum, and said: "I think to be included on the Wall of fame is a massive honour. I

Billy Whizz... England's electrically quick wing wizard Jason Robinson

have not been around in rugby union for that long and so to be included with all those other great union players is very special.

"And I think it is right that some of the players who have made this game what it is today are acknowledged in this way. It is nice that my name can be on the Wall of Fame with the rest of them."

Robinson's career may have been all too brief, but in that short time he did more than enough to take his place among some of the legendary figures in the world game.

He was helped by his wonderful relationship with Twickenham and its fabulous crowds. No fewer than 16 of his 28 tries for England were scored at Headquarters and he opened his account in his own inimitable way during his sixth appearance for his country with a four-try haul that went a long way to annihilating Romania.

During his career he scored a further two hat-tricks, one against Italy in a Six Nations match in Rome and another in the autumn of that same year, 2004, against Canada.

But never let it be said that Robinson was only potent against weaker sides. He scored the winning try against Australia in the 2003 Rugby World Cup final in Sydney, and on three occasions ran in two tries against Scotland. France also let him over their line more regularly than most, on three occasions to be precise, two of those at Twickenham, when Robinson breached Les Bleus' defences for a try in each match.

And the Leeds-born Robinson had no problem explaining his predilection for scoring tries at Twickenham. "I enjoyed playing on a big stage – and they don't come much bigger than Twickenham and playing in front of your home crowd is always a special occasion.

"The style of rugby I play as well is what lots of people want to see and what they get excited about. Although you don't play that way just for entertainment, you realise that what you are doing is exactly that, entertaining the crowd. They want to see tries.

"They don't want to see kicking all the time, they want to see some open rugby and that's what I tried to bring to English rugby union.

"I didn't try to kick, and because I was used to playing rugby league I wanted to keep a more open attacking style of play to my game and I think that certainly helped me to score so many tries at Twickenham.

"Of course I had to make adjustments over the years because of changes to the laws of the game, and I also had to become a bit smarter in the way I played, but for me it was always about getting hold of the ball and taking people on. And I think the crowd took to me because of that."

He has also appeared on a few occasions at Rugby League's adopted home in the South, Wembley. While he did not make a direct comparison between the two iconic grounds, Robinson did say: "Playing at Wembley was a childhood dream for me. I went from going down on the coach as a supporter with friends and family, to going there as a player and walking out through the tunnel and it was always a special occasion.

"But I think Twickenham is somehow different and I am not quite sure what that difference is. I think before they finished Twickenham off this summer (2008), for me there was always something missing, but now they have actually enclosed the stadium I think it just makes it into one of the best stadiums in the world.

"Beforehand, although it was a really good stadium, it just lacked a little something, but now it is the real deal for me. It is great for English rugby to have its own stadium. Wembley was always an adopted stadium for rugby league, but Twickenham was always the home of English rugby union."

The Twickenham memories are many, but for Robinson the stand-out one for him came before a ball had been passed or kicked in anger in his 24 matches there.

"My favourite personal memory of playing at Twickenham is of just standing there, singing the National Anthem, knowing that you are doing a very special job and that you have a big responsibility to serve your country well. I was always aware of that and I always wanted to do the shirt justice."

He has another reason for liking Twickenham and remembering it with fondness, indeed his recent 'final, final' appearance at HQ in the Help for Heroes match in September was a reminder of something that he always enjoyed about playing there.

"One of the things that I was really looking forward to was getting into the bath after the game. I am only a midget so I can get comfy in quite a lot of baths, but the ones at Twickenham are quite special. They are big baths. And they fill up within seconds.

"In this new era everybody is into post match ice baths and that sort of thing, but I have to say that while everybody else freezes in their ice baths I must admit I get into a bubble bath and have a good soak, even at Twickenham."

Of Robinson's 24 matches at Twickenham three stand out for the former Great Britain Rugby League international. "I think we actually played our best rugby in 2002. To have beaten Australia, New Zealand and South Africa in the autumn internationals at Twickenham before the 2003 Rugby World Cup was a very special time."

New Zealand went down 31-28, Australia 32-31 and South Africa a resounding 53-3. "I think it did wonders not just for England but for Northern Hemisphere rugby," added Robinson. "People started to think then, 'We can take these sides down as well'. It was a very significant time."

Robinson was also in the England teams which then went Down Under and beat the All Blacks 15-13 in Wellington and followed that with a 25-14 victory over the Wallabies in Melbourne as the Red Rose team built up a head of steam for their historic Rugby World Cup triumph.

For all Robinson's familiarity with Twickenham, and especially the pitch and the try lines, the former Sale Shark, admitted that he had a tendency to get 'lost' around the perimeter.

"I must admit I get lost quite a bit at Twickenham. It is such a big place and sometimes, when you come outside the West Stand after a game trying to get to another part of the ground it can be tricky, because, as you can imagine there are thousands of people outside all wanting autographs while you are walking around the perimeter. It makes trying to get from A to B then round to C very difficult, and there have been occasions where I have been trying to get somewhere and I have missed it completely and have then ended up doing a lap of Twickenham."

At least fans will now know where to find Robinson at Twickenham, on the World Rugby Museum's Wall of Fame, alongside that of fellow inductee Col Windon.

The Wallaby marked his solitary appearance on the ground, and indeed his only test against England, in memorable fashion scoring two tries in an 11-0 win over the home team.

It was a cold, wet January day but the athletic and extremely mobile Windon entertained a crowd of 70,000 with his two first half scores, which effectively sealed the match before half-time.

In all he amassed a total of 11 tries in his 20 Tests for his country, a record that was unsurpassed for three decades. Windon went on to captain the Wallabies in two tests against New Zealand in 1951. He played 26 games for New South Wales and a total of 98 for his club Randwick.

Sadly Windon died shortly before his 82nd birthday in 2003, but Australian rugby will always remember the 'Breeze' as the greatest attacking breakaway forwards in Wallaby history. The World World Rugby Museum's Wall of Fame has now endorsed that view as two more Greats go up on the wall.

Jeremy Guscott

England Centre

Born: 7.7.1965
Caps: 65
Debut: v Romania 1989
Last app: v Tonga 1999

Jeremy Guscott played in two historic games for England against South Africa. The first was as a member of the team which took on the Springboks in the year they re-entered world rugby after the end of Apartheid.

The former England and Bath centre, who played a total of 65 times for his country between 1989 and 1999, and a further eight tests for the British and Irish Lions, has very hazy recollections of that match, which England won. He did not even remember that he scored a try – the 15th of his international career – in that game.

"It was so early in my career, although I seem to remember the centre Danie Gerber played and having seen him and knowing his reputation that was the most intimidating thing about that match for me. He was in the twilight of his career and obviously therefore not as menacing as he used to be, but he was still a formidable opponent. But generally my memory of that game is not too vivid."

But Guscott, who finished with a total of 30 tries for England, had no trouble recalling another match against South Africa, in which he played (and scored) in December 1998.

It was the match where the Boks stopped, or rather, were stopped from setting a world record for consecutive wins. They arrived at Twickenham having strung together 17 victories on the trot, thereby matching the All Blacks' feat between 1965 and 1969 – as a measure of how times have changed and how few tests were played in those days, New Zealand's run spanned three years 10 months, while South Africa had amassed their 17 victories in just 16 months, a third of the time.

Nick Mallett was the mastermind behind the South African run and the Tourists were determined to notch up that magical 18th win. Guscott said: "Nick Mallett was a good guy to listen to. He spoke a lot of sense and got the team really on a roll. But it was a significant match for us for another reason as well, because Clive Woodward had not long been in charge.

"England rugby then was about going out and giving it a lash as Woodward used to say in his early days as head coach. Lawrence Dallaglio was captain, it was all incredibly exciting. Very fresh, very new."

It was certainly an exciting match, and it all ended happily for England and Guscott as well. He said: "The game will always stand out for me firstly because we ended South Africa's run, secondly because I scored a try, albeit a simple one.

"There was a cross kick to the left wing, Dan Luger palmed it down to me and I just happened to be there in support and came in and scored." That was England try number 24 for Guscott, who went on to score four against the United States Eagles and wrapped up his career with a brace against Tonga in the 1999 World Cup.

But there is another, mischievous reason why Guscott remembered the match. "All the boys remember it because it was the match in which we all took the micky out of Lawrence [Dallaglio].

"In the last two minutes of that game we were attacking towards the North Stand and something happened at a line-out; we thought we should have been awarded a penalty, but instead it was awarded to South Africa, they just tapped it and ran. The forwards were still protesting to the referee and before they knew it the ball had gone down the South African back line as far as André Snyman.

"We only realised all this after the match, when we were watching the video. But it was apparent that Lawrence had decided to give chase. He strode off like Superman, or the Incredible Hulk covering the ground with those big strides. Then suddenly, after just five paces, it was as if a sniper in the West Upper Stand had got him in his sights and had taken him out, because he stopped in his tracks.

"He wasn't injured though, it just dawned on him that he did not have a chance in hell of getting anywhere near Snyman. He spat the dummy out and lifted his arms to the skies as if to ask 'What the hell is going on?' and he just gave it up so it was left to us, in the backs to save it, which Dan Luger did. The thing is that if they had scored the try and converted it, they would have won the match by a point.

"It was also actually a nervy few moments for me, because I had shown Snyman the outside and he had taken it. There were very few occasions in my career with Bath, England or the Lions when I did that and they then got the better of me."

Guscott also recalled the after-match celebrations, a rare feat among rugby players surely.

"They were legendary," he said. "We went to Shoeless Joe's, the bar owned by former England prop Victor Ubogu, in the New King's Road. We were in the downstairs bar and caused a bit of a riot.

"So the bouncers went upstairs to tell Victor that his England rugby mates were misbehaving. Victor obviously thought it couldn't be that bad and he started to come down the stairs, but he stopped halfway down when he saw the carnage, then he turned back to the bouncers and said: "You deal with it, that's what you are paid for." And he ran away back up the stairs."

For Guscott Twickenham is a special place, encapsulating all that he feels is good in the game. He picks the 1996 Pilkington Cup final between Bath and Leicester as holding an abiding memory.

Pace and grace… the brilliant England centre Jeremy Guscott

"I was injured for that match and doing some commentary, so I went out to the West Car Park to see my family and they were having some good-natured banter with some Leicester fans and they struck a bet as to who would win.

"Long after Bath had won the family went back out to the car. The Leicester fans had all left, but there, under a windscreen wiper was a £20 note." The fact that the Leicester fans had honoured the bet in the absence of the Bath supporters and then that no one had stolen the money when it was in full public view exemplify all that is good in the game for Guscott.

As for Twickenham itself, he has only praise for the ground. "It is a wonderful stadium. It is always an occasion, always an experience."

And his elevation to the World Rugby Museum's Wall of Fame? Guscott, never one given to much emotion, is positively effusive for him. "I am pleased. Recognition such as this is nice." From someone so reticent to show their feelings, and who is imbued with modesty, and yet who has achieved so much in the game, that is quite a statement.

John Kirwan

New Zealand Wing

Born: 16.12.1964
Caps: 63
Debut: v France 1984
Last app: v South Africa 1994

John Kirwan is nothing if not generous. The moment he learned of his induction to the Twickenham Wall of Fame he started looking for ways to repay the honour.

On the face of it his solution sounded a trifle tongue in cheek. "I feel very humble," said Kirwan, at that time the head coach of Italy. "And I think the only way to repay Twickenham for this would be to bring over an Italy side and beat England on their own patch." In fact that was not to be. England won that particular match comfortably.

But the former All Black wing who scored 35 tries in 63 appearances for New Zealand did explain: "That would be the biggest honour I could bestow on England, because when that happens, when Italy win at Twickenham, it will mean that the tournament has truly come to be about six nations."

Surprisingly, given the length of his international career – 11 years between 1984 and 1994 – Kirwan only appeared at Twickenham twice. A shame given the affection and respect in which he holds Billy Williams' one time Cabbage Patch.

"When I was a youngster we used to get up at 3.00am to watch the Five Nations and Twickenham was always special even then. What it has been turned into now though is even more special. It is a celebration of rugby – 82,000 capacity and it always fills up."

The first time that Kirwan played at Twickenham it was not quite the arena it is now. He had been selected to play for an Overseas Unions XV against a Five Nations selection as part of the International Board's centenary celebrations in 1986. "In those days I think the most striking thing about Twickenham for a player was just how close the spectators were. They were almost sitting on top of the pitch."

Kirwan scored one of the Overseas team's half dozen tries as they ran out winners by 32 points to 13. "I think Grant Fox played a switch with me. Scoring at Twickenham was the fulfilment of a childhood dream."

He then had to wait a further five years before treading the hallowed turf again. On that occasion he was playing for the All Blacks in the opening game of the 1991 Rugby World Cup.

A vintage performer… New Zealand wing John Kirwan

"A really big match." New Zealand beat England 18-12, although Kirwan did not get on the scoresheet.

But as coach of Italy Kirwan has visited the stadium since and recalled grimly the match in 2001 when, with the help of a 32-point burst in 25 minutes England ran out winners by 80 points to 23.

"That was my first year as coach and that game was a turning point for us. That was the start of a long journey for us, we want to win the Six Nations, that is our goal." Hence his wish to pay back Twickenham for his elevation to the Wall of Fame; but sadly that was unfulfilled when Kirwan was the Italy coach.

Tom Kiernan   Mike Gibson

Ireland Fullback   *Ireland Centre*

Born: 7.1.1939   *Born: 3.12.1942*
Caps: 54   *Caps: 69*
Debut: v England 1960   *Debut: v England 1964*
Last app: v Scotland 1973   *Last app: v Australia 1979*

Mike Gibson and Tom Kiernan both retained sharp memories of the same England-Ireland match. It was 1970 and as Mike Gibson described it: "Tony O'Reilly's guest appearance."

Kiernan, Ireland's legendary fullback, who clocked up 54 appearances for his country at a time when there were nowhere as many opportunities to win caps, recalled: "It was the most unusual thing I experienced at Twickenham.

"We recalled Tony O'Reilly after seven years. He was to play on the wing. He arrived by chauffeur-driven car. He was Managing Director of Heinz UK at the time. He had not played since 1963 and had put on some weight in the meantime, although he was still playing for London Irish.

"There were jokes going around at the time that O'Reilly had been picked because Keith Fielding, his opposite number on the England right wing, would have to run all the way around him to get past Tony, but he really wasn't that fat."

And **Gibson** was equally sympathetic. "I roomed with Tony on that occasion. He had been criticised about playing but he still had class in his play even after seven years out of international rugby."

Sadly O'Reilly did not get much of an opportunity to make his mark on that match, which, as Gibson recalled "was a rather dour affair", Bob Hiller winning it for England with a couple of dropped goals, although Roger Shackleton scored a try late in the game.

The O'Reilly recollection aside, both these giants have something else, more significant in common. Both made their international debuts against England at Twickenham. Thereafter though their fortunes diverge.

In 1960 the portents were not good for Kiernan, who said: "When I made my Ireland debut against England in 1960 I remember it was a dark day, the Twickenham stands seemed to loom in over the pitch at us." And England ran out winners by eight points to five.

Gibson's, in contrast, was a winning appearance. "England dominated for the first ten

The consummate centre... Ireland's gifted Mike Gibson

minutes or so, which was an ideal start for me. You are under pressure but at least you are settling into the game. It allowed me to get up with the pace of the game and get used to my surroundings before being called upon to do anything positive."

Kiernan remembered the match clearly as well. "Our best game and probably the best of my career, from a team point of view, had to be the 1964 match at Twickenham, we beat England 18-5 – which in those days was translated as three goals and a try to a goal. I think I kicked three conversions."

He also recalled the young debutant. "It was Mike Gibson's first game for Ireland. It was the launch of Gibson on to the international scene and he made two or three of the tries. And he went on to become one of the greatest players of all time."

Gibson had an advantage over many debutants at HQ in that he had played there just two months previously in the 1963 Varsity Match. "There was a big crowd for that match, because in those days the teams had lots of international players so the quality of play was very high, a

On target at Twickenham to the last... Ireland fullback Tom Kiernan

fact which was recognised by spectators. That match was a most wonderful experience. The noise was the first thing that struck you as you came onto the playing area, that and the sea of faces in the East Stand.

"Simon Clarke was the Cambridge scrum-half and he was able to brief me about Twickenham because he had played for England in the Five Nations Championship earlier that year, so he led me gently into the game."

The memory was made all the sharper because Cambridge won and Gibson scored a try. So he was not inhibited when he trotted out for Ireland the following February.

"The Cambridge experience was of value to me for that Ireland game, because although it did not have the passion and pace of an international, I was prepared for the noise and the atmosphere of a full stadium. And Simon Clarke was playing scrum-half for England that day."

Finally Ireland, and crucially Gibson, got under way. He explained: "I can still picture that first try, at the end of the first half, by Noel Murphy. I came on a scissors with Jimmy Kelly on the outside. I ran inside their No8 and passed Peter Ford through the gap I had created. I went into fullback John Willcox's tackle and gave the pass, off-loaded I suppose in modern parlance – to Murphy who scored.

"I was also involved in Patrick Casey's try which began on our own 25 and was a memorable try – and a memorable victory for Ireland."

Headquarters obviously means a great deal to both men. Kiernan said: "I enjoyed playing at Twickenham, it is one of the great places to play, although I felt it was a very intimidating place, but then no international ground is friendly when you are visitors.

"The wind was always tricky there. Twickenham wasn't enclosed in those days, the North and South ends were left open, and we were not allowed to practise at Twickenham either, so you just had to try your luck as a fullback under the high ball and as a kicker.

"Although Bob Hiller, the England fullback, never seemed to have any problem there, mind you he played there more often because Harlequins used the ground for club matches."

Gibson added: "Twickenham is a very profound conveyor of memories for me. I think my first contact with rugby was the ground at Twickenham.

"My childhood was spent watching international rugby and Twickenham made the greatest impact on me. It had distinctive white boards surrounding the pitch and separating it from the spectators, and the players would go up two or three steps and through a hinged gap in the white boards to gain access to the pitch. I also remember a scoreboard which was situated in the East Stand. No other ground, to my knowledge, had one sited in a similar place."

The ground marked Kiernan's 50th cap for Ireland in 1972, a match they won, which began a run of five wins on the trot, home and away: "Sadly I played only in the first two of that run, and that was to be my last appearance at Twickenham.

"Our winning score came from the last play of the game, the try getting us in front by a couple of points. Before I took the conversion I asked the referee how much more time was left and he said it would be last kick of the match so I was very confident when I lined up what was also to be my last kick at Twickenham after seven visits to the ground." Needless to say he didn't miss the conversion.

Wilson Shaw

Scotland Outside-half

Born: 11.4.1913
Died: 23.7.1979
Caps: 19
Debut: v Wales 1934
Last app: v England 1939

Roy Laidlaw

Scotland Scrum-half

Born: 5.10.1953
Caps: 47
Debut: v Ireland 1980
Last app: v England 1988

It was a Calcutta Cup match, but not just any match between the auld enemies. This England v Scotland confrontation at Twickenham in 1938 was something very special. Indeed so special was it that it was to go down in history as the Wilson Shaw match, in honour of the stunning performance by one man.

Wilson Shaw, who went on to become President of the Scottish Rugby Union in 1970-71, set the old ground alight with as scintillating a display as you could hope to see.

And while the new stadium at Twickenham boasts crowds of 80,000 plus, just before the outbreak of the Second World War some 70,000 English and Scottish rugby supporters crammed the ground for one of the most thrilling games pre- or post-war that there has ever been.

The lead changed hands frequently. The balance of the match tilting first this way, then that. Wilson Shaw had scored the first of his two tries in the opening 40 minutes, but it was his second, three minutes from full time, which clinched the game and earned Scotland only their second victory at Twickenham.

And in between and all around those two tries Wilson Shaw was an inspiration to his men as they and their English counterparts produced a dazzling exhibition of open running rugby that kept the crowd on its toes throughout.

It is for that reason that the World Rugby Museum at Twickenham has inducted Wilson Shaw, who died in the summer of 1979, to the Wall of Fame. He should be remembered for more than one match, rugby was his life and he was justifiably and deservedly appointed CBE.

Now, remaining at Twickenham, but moving on some 45 years, and inverting the 38, you find yourself in 1983 and another landmark Scottish victory. And while the match is not remembered for any particular player, still, for one man, Scotland scrum-half **Roy Laidlaw**, it will always mean something very special.

Laidlaw will forever be associated with his Borders halfback partner John Rutherford, the pair played alongside each other on no fewer than 34 occasions out of Laidlaw's 47 Scotland appearances.

Laying down the law at No9... Scotland scrum-half Roy Laidlow

But in the 1983 Calcutta Cup match there was a moment in the game, a crucial moment, when Laidlaw ignored his partner and friend, and instead decided to go it alone. The former Jedforest scrum-half recalled with near perfect memory the second international try of his career.

"I had captained Scotland in the first three matches of what was then the Five Nations Championship and we had lost all of them." Laidlaw continued: "For the Calcutta Cup match I was demoted because they felt that it was affecting my game, but it's never one thing, is it? Jim Telfer had been appointed Lions coach so he was not allowed to coach Scotland. John Rutherford had been injured and so had missed those first three matches. So, anyway, Jim Aitken, the prop, took over the captaincy. And it turned out well. We won the game, for only the second time since the war. And I scored a try."

Actually the modest Laidlaw scored THE try. The one that mattered. The one that meant Scotland avoided the Wooden Spoon and achieved a feat that to date has not been matched – victory on English turf.

As for the try, Laidlaw remembered: "I broke off on the right-hand side at a scrum and I managed to slip past Nick Jeavons I think it was, the England flanker. I outpaced him and then cut back inside the cover defence and scored a very simple try. To score a try and win more than made up for losing the captaincy."

Laidlaw went on to work for the SRU, coaching at age group levels, helping to unearth and develop talented Scottish youngsters. A few years ago he gave that up and reverted to his trade of electrician, but he is still heavily involved in the game at his lifelong club Jedforest and at the local school.

He too has been elevated to the World Rugby Museum's Wall of Fame standing proudly with other greats of a great game.

Alessandro Troncon

Italy Scrum-half

Born: 6.9.1973
Caps: 101
Debut: v Spain 1994
Last app: v Scotland 2007

Lawrence Dallaglio

England No.8

Born: 10.8.1972
Caps: 85
Debut: v South Africa 1995
Last app: v South Africa 2007

There is an obvious Italian connection with **Lawrence Dallaglio**, who, despite his Italian father, was brought up in England, and with his mother Eileen being half English and half Irish the former Wasps back row forward had a further choice to make. He made his England debut against South Africa as a replacement in 1995.

Alessandro Troncon, Dallaglio's co-inductee on to the World Rugby Museum's Wall of Fame, made his debut a year earlier, when he too came on as a replacement – for Italy – against Spain in Parma in 1994.

Both men played against each other at Twickenham and both have fond memories of the place. In Dallaglio's case he could be accused of having 'tunnel vision' about the stadium, although it turns out to be 'tunnel love'.

"I love being in the tunnel just before a game," said Dallaglio. "You do not have to walk too far to get out on to the pitch, but when you are in it you can see and hear the crowd, which is not always the case. You only have a couple of seconds and then you are immediately out there. That was always a pretty special place for me at Twickenham."

Of course he remembered the baths, and Jason Leonard's thwarted attempt to make off with one when the old West Stand was demolished in the early 1990s.

But it is not just the ground and the baths that are special to Dallaglio. He also appreciates the people who work there, in particular the groundstaff.

"I have a lot of respect for the groundstaff," stated the former England captain. "They work tirelessly and they are good lads. They have always been helpful to me, unlocking doors, doing as much as they possibly can for me when I have trained at Twickenham. And they are always on hand to make me a nice cup of tea or coffee. They have always been brilliant."

Naturally for someone with 85 England caps and whose club Wasps has also graced the pitch at Headquarters on more than one occasion, Dallaglio has a veritable flotilla of memories of the ground.

Oddly though one of his earliest memories is not as a player, but rather as a spectator.

Italy's centurion… scrum-half Alessandro Troncon winner of 101 caps

Dallaglio took up the tale. "It was back in the days of the old Twickenham. It was 1991 and the Grand Slam decider between England and France. It was the match that had *that* try when Philippe Saint André scored at the end of a move which had begun under the France posts.

"I was in the West Stand with the rest of the England Under 19 team. We had just played Italy Under 19 the day before at Cambridge [a match the Italians won by a point] and had been given tickets for the match. We were down near the touchline in our blazers and the noise was unbelievable.

"Twickenham is a magnificent stadium now, but it was still very impressive then. I remember Brian Moore, the England hooker, coming over to take a line-out right in front of us, and he had to ask what the line-out call was a few times before he could hear it. The atmosphere was incredible that day."

By 1991 though, Dallaglio was no stranger to Twickenham. "I had been coming to Twickenham since I was kid. I played for King's House School, my prep school, across the width of the Twickenham pitch in a mini rugby tournament and I scored a try then.

"But going back to that game against France in 1991, England went on to win that game, and the Grand Slam, and that went a long way to making Twickenham a special place for me. It became something of a fortress in the late 1990s through to 2000, with memorable victories along the way against the likes of New Zealand, South Africa and Australia.

"So there have been lots of great days there for me with England, but I have to say that in a different, but remarkable way my last appearance at Twickenham was an amazing day, when I played in the Help for Heroes match. It was game that raised money for a worthy cause, watched by 55,000 people."

But Twickenham has not confined it's specialness to representative games that Dallaglio has played in. "It has also been a very special place for Wasps."

That is undeniable. On the two occasions when Twickenham has been selected to stage the Heineken European Cup final, Wasps have won the tournament.

The first time was in the 2003-04 season when they beat the previous season's European Champions Toulouse 27-20; later that season club captain Dallaglio led Wasps to a unique Twickenham double when they won the Zurich Premiership final, by beating Bath narrowly.

Wasps went on to beat Leicester in the Premiership play-off final the following season, a comprehensive 39-14 victory and the season after that they beat Llanelli in the cross border knock-out competition which was then known as the Powergen Cup.

"I think we have only lost one final at Twickenham in my time," recalled Dallaglio, "and that was in 1998 when we were beaten by Saracens."

All in all Twickenham has clearly been good to Dallaglio, even his last match there left him on a high. That was in 2008 when Wasps recorded yet another Premiership final triumph, this one a 26-16 triumph over Leicester. "If we hadn't won that game I probably wouldn't have retired," he said.

But if Twickenham has been good to Dallaglio then he has certainly been good for the ground not to mention England and Wasps. His induction on to the World Rugby Museum's

Power and passion… England's outstanding back row forward Lawrence Dallaglio

Wall of Fame is therefore not a surprise, indeed it is a natural progression.

"These days Twickenham is a phenomenal stadium and I think the Wall of Fame is a great idea," said Dallaglio. "It has ensured there is a focus on the players, although there have certainly been more than 41 great players for England. And to be included on it is worthy praise indeed."

Dallaglio's fellow inductee on to the Wall of Fame, Troncon is also worthy of inclusion. Italy may be in their Six Nations infancy when compared to the other five countries, but they are still producing fine players.

And Troncon certainly has memories of Twickenham, although his earliest one can still bring him out in a cold sweat.

Whereas the majority of inductees have warm memories of the place, especially of the famously deep, long and luxurious baths in the changing rooms, Troncon, 'Troncy', tells a very different story.

"I can remember my first match at Twickenham, very well, it was in 1996," he recalled. "And I remember the famous baths."

Troncon does not remember much about the match and would probably prefer to forget the result, a 54-21 trouncing at Headquarters, but his memories of the aftermath return to him with chilling clarity.

"When we left the pitch and went into the changing rooms I was thinking of those big baths filled with hot water, and imagining me just lying in one of them, soaking out all the aches in my muscles.

"But when we got into the changing rooms we had a shock. The baths had been filled with ice. It was the new treatment and it was supposed to be good for us we were told. The ice baths were to help us recover for our next match, which was against Scotland. So we had no choice. The manager told us we had to get in them, so I did, but I didn't enjoy it one bit. It was a shock for me."

At least Troncon was able to thaw out under a scalding hot shower afterwards, which, he said, was wonderful.

The Italy scrum-half was already an established international by then, two years into a long and distinguished career for his country during which time Troncon, who has become a legend in Italy for his feats on the rugby pitches of the world, was to win a staggering 101 caps.

And, ice baths apart, Troncon has extremely warm memories of Twickenham. "Every rugby player knows that Twickenham is the 'temple of rugby'. It is an enormous honour to have played there and now to be included on the World Rugby Museum's Wall of Fame at Twickenham it is a dream come true."

His first full international at the ground was also a dream come true for Troncon. "I had never played in a stadium like Twickenham before. It was an amazing place to me." That match sadly ended in defeat for Italy, but in personal triumph for the powerfully built Troncon, who scored the second of their three tries in the heavy defeat.

Troncon's 62nd minute effort that chill November day was the highlight of what was described at the time as an "inspiring" performance by the scrum-half; in 2005 Troncon was at

it again, scoring a try in his 'temple', although once again on that occasion Italy crashed to a heavy defeat. But given his feat of twice scoring a try on the ground it is little wonder that he feels as he does about headquarters, when he said: "Twickenham has a special place in my heart." In all, Troncon scored 19 tries for Italy.

Of course in 1996 the reconstruction and makeover of the great stadium was nowhere near complete, but for all that, the magic was still there for Troncon. And by the time he eventually decided to call time on his career, in 2007, there was just the South Stand rebuilding left to do.

But whatever the stadium looked like for Troncon the turf remained the same as he had first stepped out on a decade or so earlier. "When I had played my last game at Twickenham," recalled the Treviso-born Troncon, "and I had had a *hot* shower, and was changed, everyone else was ready to go and the manager told me to hurry up. But I said to him to wait for me, that I had something to do.

"I went out through the players' tunnel for one last time and walked out to the middle of the pitch. I had already taken lots of photographs inside, because I did not know if I would ever be back at Twickenham and in this part of the ground ever again.

"I took another 20 or so photos out on the pitch and then I put my camera away and just stood there on the pitch for a few minutes to breathe in the Twickenham air and savour the atmosphere for one final time."

Thankfully that match in 2007 was not to be Troncon's last appearance at Twickenham, as he had feared. He was back in 2009 as a member of the Italy coaching staff.

"Of course as a coach my perception of the ground is totally different from when I was a player," said Troncon, "but my feelings for the place, while different, are still as strong as when I first played at the ground."

And Troncon, like Dallaglio, now has another reason to enjoy visiting Twickenham, because the pair of them will be able to savour their place among the rugby greats on the World Rugby Museum's Wall of Fame.

Jason Leonard

England Prop

Born: 14.8.1968
Caps: 114
Debut: v Argentina 1990
Last app: v Italy 2004

The record books show that Jason Leonard scored one international try at Twickenham. In fact he was credited with another 'try' at headquarters long before that touchdown against Argentina in 1996.

It was around the time that England were due to play Canada in 1992. Twickenham was a mess of rubble during the reconstruction, Leonard was still an amateur and plying his trade as a carpenter.

Demolition of the West Stand had taken place and the man who was to become England's and the world's most capped player for a while went there in search of one of the magnificent baths from the changing rooms, Leonard having assumed that they were being thrown out.

Leonard, who was born in Barking and had joined Harlequins from Saracens, had arrived at the ground in his truck to collect a bath and explained: "They are fabulous things, a 6ft 6in guy could stretch out in them and they are about 3ft deep. But they weigh a ton. So I asked a couple of Irish builders to help me carry one from the Portakabin where they had been put and load it into the back of the van."

They had almost completed the task when Don Rutherford, the then technical director of the RFU, happened to pop his head around the corner of the van, saw what was going on and pulled the plug on Leonard's scheme by instructing the Irish workers to put the bath back in the lock-up hut.

He then turned to Leonard and said: "Nice try Jason."

Leonard, who had just recovered from a serious neck injury, a ruptured vertebra, that had required surgery and had sidelined him for six months, was subsequently selected to face Canada, and he recalled: "I had played just two games for Harlequins post op when I was called into the side."

That was a good reason to remember the match, but the fact that it was staged at Wembley because of the Twickenham makeover was another *aide mémoire*, but the third reason is the most compelling. This was the match where he first came up against one of the biggest rugby players

The lion-hearted, legendary prop Jason Leonard of England

in the world at the time, all 6ft 8in and 20st of Canada lock Norm Hadley.

"One of the England lads got on the wrong side of an early ruck, so Hadley decided to get him out of the way. I took huge exception to Hadley's method, so I threw one of the biggest punches of my life at him. He was bending down and my punch landed on his forehead. I thought ' Well that's you sorted'."

But Hadley did not appear to notice anything. Leonard watched open-mouthed as Hadley straightened up. "I just had not realised how big he was. He started to stand up, and it went on and on, so I had plenty of time to watch this egg-sized lump growing on his forehead. For my part I had a dislocated finger. When Hadley finally stood up he looked at me and asked, 'Is that all you've got Princess?' He spent the rest of the match chasing me around the pitch. Fortunately he never caught me."

The pair have since become good friends and Canada have closed the gap on the rest of the rugby world, to Leonard's obvious pleasure.

"Canada produces rugged, athletic, aggressive players of considerable ability," he said. "And

when you consider the logistics of getting all the players together from all over their vast country for a squad session, the fact they are so competitive is all the more impressive."

When Leonard made his England debut against the Pumas in 1990 he was 22 and became the youngest forward debutant for the red rose. By the time he hung up his boots 14 years later he was the first England centurion and indeed, briefly, the most capped player in the world.

By then as well he had become equally at home at loosehead and tighthead prop and had taken part in three British and Irish Lions tours. In all he played in four Rugby World Cups, from 1991 to 2003, a roller coaster ride that took him from being a part of the losing England team in the 1991 final against Australia – the lowest point of his career he has said – to the eventual World Cup winning team of 2003.

Peter Winterbottom

England Wing forward

Born: 31.5.1960
Caps: 58
Debut: v Australia 1982
Last app: v Ireland 1993

Michael Lynagh

Australia Outside-half

Born: 25.10.1963
Caps: 72
Debut: v Fiji 1984
Last app: v England 1995

Considering that **Michael Lynagh**, by his own admission, did his best to stay as far away from **Peter Winterbottom** as he could when they were in opposition, he might feel a trifle uncomfortable to find himself being inducted on to the World Rugby Museum's Wall of Fame at Twickenham alongside the former England flanker.

For Lynagh the recognition at the home of English rugby is extra special. "Twickenham featured heavily at the start of my career, when I won my second Australia cap in 1984.

"Then I appeared there at the height of my career in the 1991 Rugby World Cup final, which we won by beating England. And finally, I played the very last competitive match of my career at the ground in the Pilkington Cup final for Saracens against Wasps, which we won."

Twickenham also has a special place in Winterbottom's heart. He made his debut on the ground against the 1982 Wallabies, a match which was marked by victory for England, but memorable for Erica Roe's topless streak.

Not that Winterbottom noticed her. "Bill Beaumont was giving us the halftime captain's talk and telling us to concentrate. The only thing I noticed was a gorilla-suited person, who came onto the pitch at the other end from Erica. I was looking at him and never caught a glimpse of her."

"It was a great start to my international career being part of a victory," said Winterbottom, the former Headingley and Harlequins flanker. But another Twickenham game, despite ending in defeat for England, is what remains uppermost in his memory.

"I think the World Cup final in 1991 is a great memory and winning the first Grand Slam at the ground earlier that same year is right up there, as is the time we beat the All Blacks the following November. The place is filled with good memories for me."

Lynagh also has good memories of the place, not least the scenes in the visitors' changing rooms after that 1991 World Cup win over England.

"I was relaxing in one of the magnificent baths, with a glass of champagne. In the next bath to me was our captain Nick Farr-Jones. Suddenly your Prime Minister John Major appeared in the bathroom, accompanied by some of our officials.

Memories are made at Twickenham for England's Peter Winterbottom

Happy Days... Australia's Michael Lynagh enjoyed his Twickenham experiences

"A naked Nick stood instantly and said, 'John, good to meet you.' All the photographers around Mr Major fired off a load of shots, but that was one photo opportunity that went begging."

It was recalling that match which brought Winterbottom's name to mind and Lynagh paid tribute to him. "I always found him a wonderful competitor. He was a fantastic player. But he had a very physical presence and he was always a problem, and, as a fly-half I did try to stay away from flankers as a general rule, and from Winters in particular."

Lynagh was only on the losing side against England on two occasions. The first was in 1988, at Twickenham, the second was the more painful though when Rob Andrew's last second drop goal knocked the Wallabies out of the quarter finals of the 1995 Rugby World Cup in Cape Town.

In all Lynagh came up against England on eight occasions, three at Twickenham, the one in South Africa and in four further tests in Australia, and during that time he amassed more than a century of points, a total that includes two tries, the first of which came in his maiden match at Twickenham in 1984.

When playing for England Winterbottom did not score a try against Australia, but he did the next best thing, scoring one against the United States in Australia, during a pool match in the inaugural Rugby World Cup at the Concord Oval in Sydney in 1987. In fact on that occasion he scored two tries. There was a third and final try for Winters five years later. England were at 'home', but were playing at Wembley. Again it was a team from the North American Continent who suffered, this time it was Canada.

Colin Meads

New Zealand Second row

Born: 3.6.1936
Caps: 55
Debut: v Australia 1957
Last app: British and Irish Lions 1971

Alexander Obolensky

England Winger

Born: 17.2.1916
Died: 29.3.1940
Caps: 4
Debut: v New Zealand 1936
Last app: v Scotland 1936

Call it fate, call it spooky, or just put it down to coincidence, but it is interesting to note that in the same year that **Prince Alexander Obolensky** scored his two tries for England against New Zealand at Twickenham, **Colin Meads**, his fellow inductee on to the World Rugby Museum's Wall of Fame was born. That year was 1936.

Obolensky was a speed phenomenon. He had fled from Russia with his family in 1917 and settled in England. He was educated at Trent College and then went up to Oxford, where he won Blues as a right wing in 1935 and 1937.

When he was selected to play for England against the New Zealand All Blacks he was not even a British Citizen; citizenship was granted the following year.

But given the way he marked his international debut for his adopted country, with two dazzling tries, it is doubtful if anyone cared whether 'Obo', as he was known universally, had citizenship or not. He was an England player and had helped them record their first ever victory over the mighty All Blacks.

There was an estimated 70,000-plus crowd at Twickenham to witness the historic victory. The Prince of Wales, shortly to become King Edward VIII, was there in the Royal Box and he watched as the Prince pretty much single-handedly destroyed the Tourists.

Obolensky's first try saw him sent clear for a 40-yard dash to the line; if the first touchdown had the home supporters cheering, his second try had the All Blacks and the spectators gasping.

He received the ball when he was outside the New Zealand 25, he began heading for the right-hand corner but realising the defenders were converging on that area Obo swerved left, snaked through the remnants of the All Blacks' cover and touched down on the opposite wing.

For various reasons, including form, fitness and a dog bite, the Prince played in just three further matches, all in that winter of 1936. He did attempt to switch to the left wing in early 1937, but failed to impress the selectors.

He only survived a further four years before being killed in a flight training accident during

A hulking, physical presence... outstanding All Black lock Colin Meads

the Second World War, when his Hurricane crashed on landing and Obolensky suffered a broken neck; Colin Earl Meads has survived for a lot longer.

The All Black lock – although he won the first of his 55 New Zealand caps in the back row – was a true giant of the game, his hulking physical presence terrorising defences and dominating line-outs across three decades from 1957 to 1971.

Meads has fond memories of Twickenham from his two tests against England in 1964 and 1967, and it is little wonder they are happy memories, the All Blacks triumphed on each occasion, with 'Pinetree' Meads scoring a try against England on his first visit to Headquarters.

"To us in those days Twickenham and Cardiff Arms Park were the most famous grounds in the world. And Twickenham had baths. I remember the very first time we saw them, which was after the game against London Counties in 1964. We plunged into them with our muddy kit on that first time and were told straightaway to get out and strip off first because we had made it dirty for everyone else following us in. Those baths were fantastic, we had nothing like them in New Zealand."

Something else has stuck with the great All Black about the ground. "We had a baggage man called Matt McKenzie, a Scot, he was a brilliant guy. At halftime against England I remember for some reason the boys wanted water brought on to the pitch. I don't think it was to drink, maybe it was to wash mud off their boots, whatever.

"So Matt went off to find a container. He came up with an empty bottle of Gilbey's Gin and filled that from a tap then came out of the tunnel and up to the side of the pitch. That was as far as he got. He was stopped by an official who told him that advertising like that was prohibited and he was ordered to go back inside and remove the label. The game was so entrenched in the amateur ethos that they had to go those lengths. It was amazing."

As for his try, Meads, who scored an incredible 28 touchdowns for his country in a total of 133 games in the famous All Black jersey, is typically dismissive. "Oh, I think it came from a big forward charge. I think I got the ball from John Graham and I scored between the posts, which was useful."

Meads did not stay stuck in the past, on the contrary he welcomed progress and professionalism: "The game had to go professional because of the demands being made on players, but old fogies like me prefer the way it was in our day – long tours, four and half months to the UK for example."

However, he did not welcome his nickname Pinetree. "I got that in the Colts. We were in Japan and a couple of Taranaki players decided I looked like a guy who had worked in the local mill. He was known as Pinetree and because he had died they were able to call me by the same stupid nickname. And it stuck."

As for the legend that said he trained by running up a mountain side with a sheep under each arm, that came about because of a moment of compassion at dipping time.

"My father had said that if a sheep could not make it to the dipping then it would have to be slaughtered. I picked up these two when they could not make it up the last hill. I was being interviewed at the time by a journalist and his photographer took the picture." And the rest as they say is legend.

Now Meads and Obolensky join a host of other rugby legends on the Wall of Fame, which salutes great players who have appeared at Twickenham. No two men could be more deserving of so signal an honour.

Graham Mourie

New Zealand Wing forward

Born: 8.9.1952
Caps: 21
Debut: v British and Irish Lions 1977
Last app: v Australia 1982

Don Clarke

New Zealand Fullback

Born: 10.11.1933
Died: 29.12.2002
Caps: 31
Debut: v South Africa 1956
Last app: v Australia 1964

The myths which swirl around the exploits of **Don Clarke** focused as much on his feet as his feats.

For **Graham Mourie**, Clarke's fellow inductee on to the World Rugby Museum's Wall of Fame at Twickenham, it was his leadership, as much as his ferocious play on the flank, which commanded so much respect and awe.

The modern day game may have its giants, particularly in the forwards, but also, more pertinently in the backs, physical specimens who induce awe and inject fear into their opponents.

New Zealand All Blacks wing Jonah Lomu's impact on the world game had even the stoutest of men glancing apprehensively around them whenever he got the ball in the mid-1990s, no one will forget how he ran through seemingly frail England defenders during the 1995 Rugby World Cup in South Africa, since then the likes of Tana Umaga, another All Black have emerged.

But the big players have largely been a present day phenomenon, associated with a general increase in size in the human physique with improved medical care and vastly improved diet.

Back in the 1950s and 1960s any big man, particularly on a rugby field, would induce gasps of astonishment and induce a sense of apprehension. Not for nothing was Colin Meads, the giant All Blacks forward called Pinetree. He was huge, but he was a forward. When the New Zealanders managed to produce a gargantuan back, that was when eyes widened.

For a long time Clarke's 6ft 2in 17st frame made him the largest back in All Blacks history, not to mention around the world at that time, even in his schooldays, although his precocious growth spurts saw him barred from rugby football and forced to take up netball.

But he still managed to play club rugby for Kereone third grade (under 18) when he was still only 12 years of age.

If his physical presence aroused fear in opposition sides, his goal-kicking feats had them positively trembling with trepidation if any member of their side were penalised within 60 yards of the goalposts.

An astute captain and fierce competitor… New Zealand flanker Graham Mourie

They knew that, unless a freak gust of wind sprang up, or a fly got in his eye at a crucial moment, or he lost his footing when delivering the *coup de grâce*, they would almost certainly be three points down once the kick had been taken.

Clarke was a toe-punter, using the old-fashioned toe of the boot end-on to propel the heavy rugby balls of that era prodigious distances. Successful kicks at goal from the halfway line were almost a given where Clarke was concerned.

Not that he needed to wear boots, if legend is to be believed. There are those who swear that Don Clarke used to practise kicking barefoot and that he landed kicks regularly from 50 yards with no protective footwear – and no broken bones.

In the summer of 1963 Clarke clinched a narrow victory for the All Blacks over a touring England team in Christchurch by landing a 65-yard goal from a mark, so by the time he arrived at Twickenham on the All Blacks 1963-64 tour some six months later, his reputation had gone before him. So had his nickname 'The Boot'.

Big boots and great feats… All Black fullback Don Clarke

There were no monster kicks, but, as dull as the match was Clarke opened the scoring with a 46-yard penalty, followed that up with a second from half that distance and then converted David Graham's try.

Despite a career dogged by injury Clarke scored a total of 781 points in his 89 appearances for the All Blacks – 31 of them Test matches – a record which stood until 1988 when Grant Fox surpassed that figure.

He emigrated to South Africa in the 1970s and died of cancer in December 2002 at the age of 69.

He co-inductee Mourie was a classic case of a man who led by example. And what an example.

Under his captaincy the 1978 All Blacks created a slice of Rugby Union history by becoming the first touring New Zealand team to complete a Grand Slam against the four Home Countries.

The All Blacks arrived at Twickenham for the Armistice Day fixture on the back of close wins over Ireland and Wales.

Under the astute captaincy of Mourie, an outstanding back row forward who had a solid work ethic and deep-seated sense of fair play, the New Zealanders demonstrated a near water-tight defence – they conceded just one try in their four internationals – and relied on a solid pack which featured Brad Johnstone, the former Italy coach at loosehead prop. Indeed Johnstone scored the All Blacks' second try against England from a line-out a yard from the line.

An ineffectual England side was perhaps lucky not to have conceded more points, thankfully even the New Zealanders proved human with lapses of concentration and the odd poor decision with the try-line seemingly at their mercy.

The striking quality of this All Blacks party though was not their ability to win, but rather the spirit in which they approached and played each match. In addition to the Grand Slam, this tour was marked by the New Zealanders' sense of sportsmanship, which can be placed squarely at Mourie's feet. He showed you could win nicely.

Mourie captained his country in 19 of his 21 tests, losing just four matches – two to France and two to Australia and no more worthy candidate could have been inducted on to the World Rugby Museum's Wall of Fame.

Tony O'Reilly

Ireland Centre

Born: 7.5.1936
Caps: 29
Debut: v France 1955
Last app: v England 1970

Keith Wood

Ireland Hooker

Born: 27.1.1972
Caps: 58
Debut: v Australia 1994
Last app: v France 2003

Neither of the latest inductees on to the World Rugby Museum's Wall of Fame at Twickenham could be blamed for harbouring miserable memories of Twickenham, because neither Irishman, **Dr Sir Tony O'Reilly** nor **Keith Wood**, ever tasted victory at England's HQ, when wearing the green jersey of their country.

O'Reilly, a powerfully-built and prolific scorer of tries on the wing, surprisingly never broached the Red Rose defences, home or away, and he experienced four defeats at Twickenham, including his final appearance in 1970.

That was still a notable match for the brilliant businessman and former chairman of Heinz. His previous appearance in an Ireland shirt had been seven years earlier in the victory over Wales in Cardiff. That set a record in the Northern Hemisphere for the longest international career, 16 seasons.

Even though he did not score on St Valentine's Day in 1970, O'Reilly still managed to make his mark on the fixture. Ireland's legendary lock, another Ireland inductee onto the World Rugby Museum's Wall of Fame, Willie John McBride recalled: "... he turned up at training the week before the match in a chauffeur-driven Rolls Royce. He even got the chauffeur to carry his kit into the changing room."

O'Reilly though has legendary status in the Rugby World, holding the record of having scored six tries in his 10 Lions' test appearances. He touched down four times in 29 tests during his distinguished Ireland career which spanned three decades from 1955 to 1970.

The former Old Belvedere, Leicester and London Irish player O'Reilly is joined on the Wall of Fame by another legendary figure in Irish and world rugby.

Former hooker Keith Wood did not have to suffer quite as long a torment as did O'Reilly, but even so he found his two appearances in an Ireland shirt at Twickenham to be just as painful. Indeed, Wood's defeats at Twickenham were not confined to internationals, as he recalled.

"I would have to describe Twickenham as a monument to my despair, because I haven't won

A Rolls Royce among centres… Ireland's richly talented Tony O'Reilly

there. I have been beaten in two cup finals, the Heineken Cup and the Tetley's Bitter Cup in 2001."

Yet Wood insisted: "I have very fond memories of my first time at Twickenham. It was in 1994, when Ireland beat England and Simon Geoghegan scored in the corner. I didn't play, I sat on the bench.

"The bench in those days was in the old West Stand, it was a rickety, old, wood-panelled part of the stadium. I've a feeling it was in front of the Royal Box. I remember I had to keep limiting my enthusiasm for jumping up and down, because I was sitting right in front of Prince Charles; my language was not the best I think.

"There is a spliced photograph of that day, it was taken by the Irish doctor. He put together two photographs of the changing room after the win. It was very atmospheric; it's kind of sepia-toned, even though it is a modern-day photograph. It's an unbelievable photo.

"There is steam rising off the baths and steam coming off the Irish players, who are strewn

Twickenham, a monument to his despair... Ireland hooker Keith Wood

all over the place. I am in one corner, and nobody, *nobody*, knows it is me. No one twigs that the player sitting in the background of that photograph is me. I look totally different, at that time I had a full head of black hair, and no-one recognises me at all.

"I look at the guys who were playing in the Ireland team then and there were some really good guys playing for Ireland in the 1990s. There are a lot of great memories in that photograph.

"And the fact that I never came off the bench does not detract from the pleasure I got from being a part of that day. In some ways it made even sitting on the bench seem unbelievably important. You haven't played, you haven't been involved, but you have been really touched by the essence of that victory. And I can tell you that on that day without a shadow of a doubt, I was a part of that victory. I thought it was phenomenal. I was 22."

His debut was to follow later that year on Ireland's tour of Australia. There was another metamorphosis in Wood's career that summer Down Under, apart from moving up from benchman to fully fledged international, Wood was also transformed physically, into the more readily recognisable shaven-headed figure the rugby world came to know.

"It was that year, 1994 that one of our props Gary Halpin, shaved my head. Gary was bald and I think he wanted someone to share his shame, so he shaved my head. I got kicked in the face in the first match after that and I got two black eyes, which earned me the nickname of Uncle Fester, after the character in the television programme the Addams family. And it stuck."

So did defeat. The one in 2000 was particularly bad. Ireland were thrashed by England and conceded 50 points for the first time in an international. And there was some personal pain and indignity for Wood as well, from his fellow Harlequin, the England prop Jason Leonard.

"The other memory I have of Twickenham is sparked by a picture I have in my house. It was taken during the match in 2000. It shows the England flanker Richard Hill, who is kind of on the ground with me, having half-tackled me, and the prop Jason Leonard is literally strangling me. He has me in a headlock, and the skin of my neck is halfway up my face, it looks like I am being given a facelift. He is choking me.

"And at another stage in that same match Jason kicked me in the head at a ruck. I got up and tottered around a bit and Jason walked over to the referee, Derek Bevan of Wales, and said, 'Referee, I think that player is concussed.' Thankfully I did not have to go off and I played on. I got my revenge, I did a knee drop on him later in the game.

"The previous week I'd been hanging off him in the Harlequins front row. He had looked after me as one of my props for seven years at Quins, and because of that, I think, he decided to kick the living shit out of me on the Twickenham turf."

It did not get much better that year either. Wood found himself at Twickenham once more as a member of the Munster team that was contesting the Heineken Cup final against Northampton.

"That year, 2000, I had what I often describe as my worst and best moments in rugby.
"I played for Munster against Northampton in the Heineken Cup final at Twickenham. It was a tense, tight game. A hard game. The ground was really greasy. There were kicks being put over and kicks being missed. And we lost 9-8.

"We were absolutely gutted and we started walking towards the South Stand where there seemed to be a lot of Munster supporters. It was maybe 30 or 40 seconds after the final whistle when suddenly the crowd started to sing 'The Fields of Athenry'. And the whole crowd joined in. There was a level of empathy between the Munster players and the crowd and I put it down as one of the best moments that I have ever experienced in rugby.

"Even though we had lost the final, a bond had been forged between the Munster players and the supporters that day at Twickenham. It was only going to be a matter of time before that led to a Heineken Cup victory for Munster, because … it was unbelievable.

"It was the start of the Munster thing; it was a journey that was beginning. The number of supporters was beginning to swell."

A year later and there was more disappointment at Twickenham. "I was playing for Harlequins and we had reached the Tetley's Bitter Cup final. A touch judge gave a totally wrong decision awarding a line-out to Newcastle and they scored off the throw in the corner, to win the match. I couldn't believe it. We had not taken the ball into touch, they had. That was so bitter, excuse the pun."

At least Wood had the satisfaction of scoring a critical try in the delayed Six Nations match in October of that year – the fixture had to be put back because of the foot and mouth outbreak. The victory ensured Ireland not only beat England but denied them a Grand Slam. Unfortunately that game was played at Lansdowne Road.

Wood is not one to dwell on negatives. Far from it, he also remembered some rare and precious moments spent with two legendary actors, Richard Harris and Peter O'Toole at Twickenham.

Harris, a former rugby player from Munster, was particularly fanatical about his province and their fortunes on the rugby field, unfortunately, his presence was not exactly welcome in the Munster dressing room.

"Richard Harris was at school with my old man [prop Gordon Wood, who won 29 caps for Ireland from 1954 to 1961, and played in two tests for the 1959 Lions. He died in 1982].

"They were in school together for five years. We used to call Harris 'Jonah', because every time he came in to see us we'd lose. He brought his own dark cloud with him, and it was terrible, because all he ever wanted was for us to win."

Not even the presence of O'Toole could leaven the outcome of Munster's matches, although the two actors certainly provided some entertainment for the players.

"Harris would bring O'Toole into the changing room. We never knew how they got in, but there they'd be, in the dressing rooms, they would just be there, part of the furniture. They were a couple of fantastic old rogues. I had a chance, after one match at Twickenham, to sit down and have a chat with Peter O'Toole and it was just fantastic. He told some great stories."

Chris Oti

England Wing

Born: 16.6.1965
Caps: 13
Debut: v Scotland 1988
Last app: v Italy 1991

George Stephenson

Ireland Centre

Born: 22.12.1901
Died: 6.8.1970
Caps: 42
Debut: v France 1920
Last app: v Wales 1930

The England rugby anthem Swing Low Sweet Chariot ends with an 'o' and a 't', but it also began with an 'o' and a 't'. The year was 1988 and Ireland were at Twickenham. And so was a certain Cambridge University student.

The 'o' and 't' in question was the then England winger **Chris Oti**. It was his second appearance in an England shirt and he marked his Twickenham debut in spectacular style by scoring a hat-trick.

The grace and pace of the Wasps threequarter as he helped himself to the three touchdowns in the second half of a remarkable game that sadly marked the end of Nigel Melville's brilliant test career, caught the rugby public's fancy and imagination and prompted a section of the crowd to begin singing the spiritual after Oti's second try.

The song had been adopted in rugby clubs the length and breadth of England, and had to be sung in accompaniment to a series of suggestive (and in some cases downright crude) gestures. It invariably wound up being hummed to the various hand signals. Fortunately it was the spirit of the song and not its crudity that appealed on that March afternoon 16 years ago.

These days Oti, who won just 13 caps, the last of them against Italy in the 1991 Rugby World Cup, is reluctant to step into the limelight and give interviews.

But in a previous chat he did admit: "I don't think I ever fulfilled my potential. I felt I could have done a lot better. But the hat-trick was a marvellous thing to have achieved."

Whether he should have received more recognition and more caps is immaterial, but at least Oti has not been forgotten by the game. He has been inducted on to the Twickenham Wall of Fame – a signal honour accorded to players from all over the world who have played at Twickenham and who have further marked that appearance with something special.

No one can ever doubt that Oti's hat-trick was not something special. Until Oti's first try England had not scored a try in their three previous Championship matches. In addition to Oti's treble there were two tries for the other wing Rory Underwood, the second of which was absolute cracker.

England's 'Charioteer'… hat-trick king Chris Oti

Oti has always played down his own contribution, claiming: "Rory scored two brilliant tries." True, but Oti's were also very special. When previously questioned something else mattered more to him about the occasion. "I think that I contributed something else that day," said Oti, the first black player since James 'Darkie' Peters (1906-07) to wear and England shirt.

"That was a self-belief among the players. When we started scoring tries they came so easily and England certainly went on to achieve greater things."

Twickenham was also special, but for entirely different reasons, for his fellow inductee on to the World Rugby Museum's Wall of Fame, Ireland's **George Stephenson**.

Stephenson was captain of his country when they turned up at English HQ in February 1929, never having previously won there. They had beaten England at Blackheath, Leeds, Richmond and Leicester, but victory at Twickenham had eluded them, although they did make a promising start in the ground's opening season, with a draw in 1910, a result they managed to repeat on Valentine's Day in 1925.

So on that February day in 1929 they were eager to go one better. And they did open the scoring but the Irish then slipped behind when England scored a converted try while centre Stephenson was off – no replacements temporary or permanent in those days – to be treated for a rib injury.

History man... George Stephenson led Ireland to first Twickenham victory

But they bred them tough in those days. Although the injury was painful enough to rule him out of the next match against Scotland, Stephenson returned to the field of play against England, and that was just as well, because after he had returned the Irish scored a second try.

And when England, with time rapidly running out, pressed hard for the winning score it was Stephenson's last ditch tackle on Cambridge University student Robert Smeddle which prevented a try and helped them to record their first victory at Twickenham.

Ken Jones
Wales Wing

Born: 30.12. 1921
Died: 18.4.2006
Caps: 44
Debut: v England 1947
Last app: v Scotland 1957

Phil Bennett
Wales Outside-half

Born: 24.10.1948
Caps: 29
Debut: v France 1969
Last app: v France 1978

The sporting achievements of these two Welsh inductees on to the World Rugby Museum's Wall of Fame are huge and impressive. Both were all-rounders – **Ken Jones** was a sporting all-rounder, an Olympic medallist, who won Commonwealth and European sprinting honours as well. Jones also used his speed to help Wales to a couple of Grand Slams in 1950 and 1952.

And one of his 17 tries in 44 appearances in a Wales jersey helped pull off the historic victory over the New Zealand All Blacks in 1953.

The other inductee, **Phil Bennett**, was the complete, the all-round, fly-half, a man who conjured up tries and wins for Wales with astonishing regularity during an international career which spanned 10 seasons between 1969 and 1978.

In that time Bennett experienced the glory of two Grand Slams, tasted the triumph of four Triple Crowns, and of course both men had their days at Twickenham, which is why they have been honoured with elevation to the World Rugby Museum's Wall of Fame.

Oddly, while many Englishmen remember Bennett for the three penalties he kicked at HQ to win the Five Nations match and help Wales to the Grand Slam in 1976 – "I thought Allan Martin kicked one of those," he said, his memory playing tricks with him – in fact the match which remains his favourite came much earlier than that. At the beginning of the previous decade to be precise, when a callow, 15-year-old Bennett travelled to Twickenham as a member of a Wales Schoolboy team to take on their English counterparts.

"It was quite a trip for us," recalled Bennett. "I lived in Felinfoel, the village where I was born, just outside Llanelli and there I was, heading for London. It was a fantastic feeling for a young Welsh boy to know I would be playing at this great stadium.

"Although memories of the match are vague we did beat England and I contributed to the win by landing a 45-yard drop goal.

"To this day I do not know where I got the strength to kick the ball that far, in those days they were big, heavy balls which got even more heavy when they got wet.

Mercurial runner and midfield maestro… Wales fly-half Phil Bennett

"I was playing at fly-half and the player marking me was a teenage flanker who was to go on and win caps for England, Tony Neary.

"It was played on a Wednesday and in the evening there was a sports programme on television introduced by Peter Dimmock and our win and my drop goal was mentioned on that.

"We travelled back to Wales and the following day there was a report on the match in the Daily Express, written by their correspondent Pat Marshall and my father cut the article out of the paper.

"When I went for a walk in the village everyone said they had seen me on TV the previous night and that it was a great drop goal. I felt like a superstar. It was a great experience for a youngster.

"At school two of the teachers said how well the team had done, and Derek Quinnell, who had been a reserve for the match, and I were singled out for congratulations."

Bennett still lives within shouting distance of Felinfoel, around half a mile outside the village, but he is known for his exploits all over the Rugby world.

The victory over England at Twickenham in February 1978 laid the foundations for an incredible third Slam of that decade, which was achieved against France in a thrilling game at Cardiff Arms Park a month later.

In contrast to that thrilling introduction to Twickenham, Bennett recalled that it was a poor match. "It was bitterly cold and raining," said the former British Lion.

"Alastair Hignell kicked two penalties for England, and the reason I thought Allan Martin had kicked one of our three was because he always used to ask to take the long kicks.

"But when we were awarded a penalty very late in the game, with the score level at 6-6, I did not hear Allan asking to take the kick, that one was left for me."

He landed the kick and after the France match hung up his boots. But Bennett had shared in a far more convincing victory over England at Twickenham two years earlier, when again they completed the Grand Slam.

It was a match he had not originally been picked for after falling foul of the 'Big Five' the Wales selectors, after aggravating an ankle injury which had originally kept him out of a Wales trial match precisely to avoid re-injuring himself. He was axed from the squad, only to be recalled at a very late stage after the first and second choices at fly-half, John Bevan and David Richards were themselves injured.

Although Bennett did not get on the scoresheet that day his pass sent in JPR Williams for the fullback's second try as Wales ran up what was their highest winning margin at Twickenham at that time.

Bennett's memories of the old stadium are headed by the baths. "They were wonderful, big things," he said. "It was great just to lie in one of those baths filled with boiling hot water, for half an hour after a hard match on a cold day.

"And the atmosphere at Twickenham was wonderful. The crowd never tried to put me off my goal kicks by making a noise. And I never felt intimidated by the crowd even though they were practically within touching distance of the pitch.

"When you went to collect the ball after it had been kicked into touch someone in the crowd would invariably say something."

But unlike so many players who played at Twickenham before the ground underwent its transformation into one of the finest rugby stadia in the world, Bennett feels the redevelopment has not spoiled Twickenham for him.

"I think it has kept a lot of its character. It's a lovely stadium. These days when I am doing my broadcasting work I love to go into one of the bars for a pre-match shandy and just take in the atmosphere there. It is great, it still has a certain sparkle."

Sparkle was something that **Ken Jones**, Bennett's fellow inductee on to the World Rugby Museum's Wall of Fame, brought to the matches he played in a couple of decades earlier.

His career began against England and he certainly had a memorable match or two. In 1948, as the Five Nations creaked into action following the Second World War it was a second half try by Jones which ensured a draw at Twickenham.

But his best match on English soil came four years later when Wales, who had lost Bleddyn

Feats of Olympian stature... Wales flying winger Ken Jones

Williams with flu on the morning of the match, pretty soon found themselves trailing 6-0.

But a brilliant break by Cliff Morgan set up Jones who sprinted through and in the second half Jones clinched victory with his second try.

In all, that season Jones scored four tries in the Championship as Wales swept through unbeaten and he was an ever present, to the extent that he made a record 43 consecutive appearances for Wales.

But the Blaenavon-born Jones, who died in April 2006, always reckoned his finest sporting moment was on the athletics track when the British sprint relay team finished with a silver medal in the 1948 Olympics.

The quartet was originally awarded gold after it was deemed that the United States team had messed up its first baton change, but that was rescinded on appeal so Jones ended up with silver.

Even so his exploits on the rugby fields of the world live on, and none more so than those on the famous stage that is Twickenham.

Wavell Wakefield

England Wing forward

Born: 10.3.1898
Died: 12.8.1983
Caps: 31
Debut: v Wales 1920
Last app: v France 1927

Philippe Saint-André

France Wing

Born: 19.4.1967
Caps: 69
Debut: v Romania 1990
Last app: v South Africa 1997

The try which France conjured up in the Grand Slam decider at Twickenham in 1991 has passed into the legend and lore of the game. It was scored by **Philippe Saint-André** and brought the stadium to its feet in 1991.

But despite having made that historic and stunning touchdown, Saint-André has reason not to remember the stadium too fondly. "You know for all that I have wonderful memories of Twickenham, it is after all the temple of rugby for me, yet there is the bad memory of losing every time I played there," confessed Saint-André.

"I have won with France in every stadium in the world, from New Zealand and Australia to South Africa, Edinburgh and Cardiff, but never at Twickenham.

"But that try was special. Mind you so was the French team that year. I was young and I was surrounded by some wonderful players, especially in the backs, where we had Serge Blanco, Jean-Baptiste Lafond, Franck Mesnel, Philippe Sella, Didier Cambérabéro and Pierre Berbizier at scrum-half."

The try began behind the French line after Simon Hodgkinson missed a penalty kick. Berbizier caught the ball, stood for a moment then lobbed the ball to Blanco who was looping round behind him. Lafond and Cambérabéro took the ball on, found Sella out on the right, he momentarily held it up waiting for the support to arrive, then back it went to Cambérabéro who chipped ahead, re-gathered, then launched a cross kick to the middle of the field where Saint-André was storming through, he collected the ball with barely a pause and crossed for the try. It had the whole of the stadium in uproarious appreciation of a special moment in the game and ranks today with the famous Barbarian score of 1973 as one of the greatest tries scored.

France scored a total of three tries to England's one yet still lost, they slipped in the World Cup later that year, and, although two years after that Saint-André scored two tries in the Five Nations match, still he finished on the losing side. He experienced defeat again when he was captain in 1995. It was not until after Saint-André had won the last of his 69 caps and retired that France finally won at Twickenham, in 1997.

Laying down the lore… scorer of a legendary try, Phillip Saint André

But like his co-inductee **Wavell Wakefield**, the French winger made enough of an impression at the ground and embodied all that is good in the game, to endear himself to rugby lovers the world over.

Wakefield, who played his club rugby for Harlequins, was born in Beckenham in Kent and attended Sedbergh School before going up to Cambridge. He won rugby Blues in 1921, when the Light Blues lost to Oxford, then captained Cambridge to victory in 1922. That was the first year that players wore numbers on their backs. In early 1923 he captained the Royal Air Force to wins over the Army and the Royal Navy. By the late Spring he had tasted Grand Slam glory with England under the leadership of W J A 'Dave' Davies and then himself captained England to the Grand Slam in 1924 – the second time they had achieved back-to-back slams following the triumphs of 1913 and 1914. Wakefield had already enjoyed Grand Slam success with England in the 1921 season. He went on to captain his country on 13 occasions.

In all he won 31 caps in the England back row, and in fact he has been credited with having re-invented the role of the flanker, which had not been such a mobile position until his arrival.

A born leader... former England captain Wavell Wakefield

After retirement from the game in 1930 he went on to carve himself a distinguished career in politics, getting elected as a Conservative MP for Swindon in 1935 – in the 1945 General Election he switched to Marylebone in London. He was knighted in 1944, and on retiring from Parliament in 1963 was gazetted the first Baron Wakefield of Kendal.

Throughout his political career he remained involved with Rugby and went on to become the 42nd President of the Rugby Football Union in 1950, and from 1950 to 1980 was also president of his club Harlequins.

Agustin Pichot

Argentina Scrum-half

Born: 22.8.1974
Caps: 73
Debut: v Australia 1995
Last app: v France 2007

There are a number of reasons why Twickenham stadium is etched indelibly on the memory of Agustin Pichot, but oddly one reason stands out.

It happened this way. Pichot, Argentina's brilliant scrum-half and former captain, had decided to buy a couple of things in the RFU Shop at Headquarters before the Pumas took on England in November 2000.

Naturally enough there was quite a queue, which the former Argentina captain dutifully joined. Now the thing about Pichot is that he is one of the most easily recognisable players because of his shoulder length, jet black hair, a feature that certainly makes him stand out from the crowd. Well usually. But not on this occasion.

In front of him was a father and his son, and they were discussing the forthcoming clash. Pichot takes up the tale. "Eventually they began to talk about me. Then they turned around and, assuming that I was an Argentinian fan, they began talking to me about the Pumas scrum-half Agustin Pichot.

"They said to me: 'What do you think about Agustin Pichot?' And I said that yeah I thought he was OK. We ended up talking about myself for about 15 minutes. And they never once recognised me.

"There was even a picture of me in a Barbarian jersey up on one of the walls in the shop. I left without telling them who I was. I thought it was very funny."

The result of that match was not quite so amusing though. England won it without conceding a single point, leaving Argentina's record against England at Twickenham at three defeats out of their three appearances at that point.

It was not until their fourth visit to Twickenham, in 2006, that the Pumas finally reversed the trend, creating a little bit of rugby history in the process and leaving Pichot, who was captain on that day, with one of his greatest memories of the ground.

Appropriately enough the match took place on Remembrance Day, the 11th day of the 11th

The proudest of Pumas... Argentina's doughty scrum-half Agustin Pichot

month. It is certainly a day every Argentine rugby fan and player will remember as well. It was the day that the Pumas savaged the then World Champions and emerged with their maiden victory against England on English soil.

Argentina had twice tasted victory over England in previous meetings, but on both occasions they were on home turf in Buenos Aires, in 1990 and again in 1997.

And this victory was extra special, because it was the first time England had lost at Twickenham to a country that was not in the so-called 'top nine' rugby playing nations.

"I had always dreamed that one day Twickenham would be the stage for an amazing moment in Argentine rugby," said Pichot, who pronounced himself delighted to have been inducted on to the World Rugby Museum's Wall of Fame.

It was certainly that. It also helped Argentina's case to be embraced as one of the top rugby playing nations in the world. Their third place finish in the Rugby World Cup a year later reinforced the impression that the Pumas had finally come of age and were ready to join the big boys.

"That victory was like a point where everything converged, all the fight for recognition, for bringing Argentina to a place where we deserved to be," said Pichot with understandable pride.

"I remember the game perfectly. I missed a tackle on Paul Sackey and he went on to score a try. I remember Federico Todeschini's interception try and that won us the game. I remember receiving the man of the match award – I couldn't believe it.

"The game was very physical as usual, England were suffering from a bad run of games but the pride of the English was still there. The press were against them but they still came out and they played a very physical game. But we were very well prepared, we were ready to perform.

"Everything just fell into place. It wasn't just because it was a match that we had won, it was more special than that. There was a magic in the air.

"My first thoughts when the final whistle went were that it was the second special moment of my career. Now I have three special moments. The first was when I pulled on the Pumas jersey for debut against Australia in 1995; the second was beating England in 2006, the third was Argentina finishing in third place in the 2007 Rugby World Cup."

Typically though Pichot has realised that the victory was bigger than one player, even though he was the Pumas' captain. The passionate Pichot wants to see Argentina competing on a more regular basis with the likes of Australia, New Zealand and South Africa, turning the present Tri-Nations into a quadrangular tournament. For that reason the 2006 triumph was crucial.

"I think it was a marker for us. There is a thing in rugby, you almost have to pass an exam, like at school. You have to achieve things and it is not just a question of achieving something, but also a matter of how you achieve it.

"One of the most difficult things a national rugby team has to do before it can enter the world of the big guys, is to beat England at Twickenham. Not many countries have done it.

"Argentina have only played a handful of games at Twickenham, maybe five times in the last 20 years so for a player moments like that are rare. At the moment for Argentina it is a one-off, victory over England at Twickenham. Which we achieved on the 11th November. I could not forget the date.

"For me Twickenham is very special, I played more than 70 games in my international career, I toured a lot, and I have been to some wonderful stadiums in places such as New Zealand and South Africa, but I have a very special feeling for Twickenham.

"For one year, when I was playing for Richmond, I lived just 200 metres from Twickenham."

And he is one of a great many players to have graced the home of English rugby who is an admirer of the legendary baths, although for Pichot something that impresses him even more is the pitch itself.

"The grass and how they take care of it. It is very tidy it is well taken care of."

Pichot, who has been working for the Argentine government on various projects since retiring from the game, is something of an Anglophile, having played club rugby first for Richmond then Bristol, where he honed his skills in the competitive English Premiership.

"England is my second country, my second home. I went to university in England, I played club rugby for six years in England. I was very young when I first arrived, but the English people gave me everything.

"So in 2006 when the final whistle went, all these thoughts went through my head. All the times that I had walked by the ground, all the moments that I had lived in England and had enjoyed there. England was one of the countries that had helped me achieve that victory, it was like being in the garden of my house with my big brother saying to me 'Well done'.

"I paid respect to the whole concept of me having been embraced by the English people, and for being given the chance, that is how it seemed to me, to be able to come back and say to England and the English people, this is how much I have evolved in the game, and it is thanks to you."

Pichot, who is fluent in Spanish, English, French and Italian, is probably destined for some sort of ambassadorial role for his country, having already played a part in helping to get Rugby Sevens accepted for the 2016 Olympic Games, which will be staged in soccer-mad Brazil.

His passion for his country and his sport is apparent. He is eager to spread the word and have Rugby Union played by more South American countries.

"It is brilliant that Rio de Janeiro is to host the 2016 Olympic Games," he said, "because it is good for South America, and it is good for rugby itself that it too will be in the 2016 Games.

"It will be great for the region, because apart from Argentina and Spain, only Uruguay and Chile play rugby, the rest of the countries are very football orientated. With the Games coming to Rio and including rugby, it will be wonderful for the whole sport."

Pichot has clearly got his career mapped out. Whether he ends up as a diplomat, or even perhaps a politician, he has already taken the initial steps. "I am not in the external affairs department of the government, but I am doing some work for different government departments. I have been doing this for the last year." And no doubt for many years to come. But whatever he ends up doing, Rugby will always hold an important place in his heart. As will Twickenham.

"I think Twickenham is the cathedral of rugby. So everything that takes place there is special. It is a sacred place. It is the soul of rugby. The place is magic.

Dean Richards

England No.8

Born: 11.7.1963
Caps: 48
Debut: v Ireland 1986
Last app: v Ireland 1996

Dean Richards' reluctance to seek the limelight can reach almost pathological levels. He is the archetypal team man and throughout an international career that embraced 48 caps for England and half a dozen appearances for the British and Irish Lions has shrugged off praise and honours consistently. It is not false modesty or feigned humility, it is simply that fame on a personal level is just not his scene.

But his achievements on the rugby fields of the world make him well qualified to take his place on the World Rugby Museum's Wall of Fame at Twickenham.

And with his mop of fair hair, jersey more often than not hanging outside his shorts and most famously of all, his socks rolled down to his ankles, it is unlikely that few will ever forget Richards, least of all the Italians who contested the 1991 World Cup.

It was his only brush with Italy and it was a feisty match at Twickenham and a game he does not recall with fondness. Nevertheless time has softened him enough for him to allow that, after what he felt was a cynical approach more than a decade ago that the 'Sixth Nation' has come a long way in the intervening years.

"They have improved hugely since that 1991 World Cup match," said the Leicester legend, at one time the world's most capped No8, consigning the memories to his mental waste paper basket.

Oddly a rubbish bin features in one of his lasting memories of Twickenham. If, in years to come, there is puzzlement in the sporting memorabilia market over the rarity of 1996 Pilkington Cup runners-up tankards and questions get no answers, investigators need look no further than Richards for an explanation.

Tigers had just lost out by a point after referee Steve Lander awarded a last minute penalty try against them and Neil Back had just shoved the match official in the back.

Richards entered the dressing room clutching his runners-up memento, a glass tankard. He spotted a large rubbish bin and lobbed the tankard in the direction of the receptacle. The

The archetypal team man... England No8 Dean Richards

intention was for it symbolically to drop into the bin, testimony to what Richards thought of the match, the referee and the day.

Unfortunately it hit the side of the bin, dropped to the floor where, in front of the rest of the Leicester team, it shattered into hundreds of pieces.

"All the other players thought I had deliberately thrown it at the wall and most of them followed suit before I could stop them. I doubt there are more than one or two of those tankards around now."

He does have far more pleasant memories of Twickenham – old Twickenham, "There was an intimacy to the old stadium, with spectators just half a dozen feet from the touchline. I don't think any other international stadium had that intimacy" – as well.

"I remember the back-to-back Grand Slams we clinched there in 1991 and 1992. In fact that first Slam against France we won after having gone behind and they scored that fantastic try counter attacking from behind their own line."

Now Richards' induction on to the Wall of Fame – "It is a great honour for me but there are many others who deserve it more than me." – will jog a few more memories of this icon of late 20th Century English rugby.

Rob Andrew

England Outside-half

Born: 18.2.1963
Caps: 71
Debut: v Romania 1985
Last app: v Wales 1997

Mircea Paraschiv

Romania Scrum-half

Born: 1954
(no official record of precise date of birth)
Caps: 62
Debut: v Spain 1975
Last app: v France 1987

Romania holds a special place in **Rob Andrew's** international Rugby Union career, marking as it does a hat-trick of firsts for the former England and Lions fly-half.

Andrew's induction to the Wall of Fame at Twickenham is a reflection of all that he has achieved in, and done for, the game in more than two decades of playing and coaching.

His first major tour, in 1982 was with England Under 23 – to Romania; in 1985 he made his England debut against – Romania; in 1989 in Bucharest he captained England for the first time against – Romania.

"There is no doubt that Romania has played a big part in my rugby life," admitted Andrew.

"I remember when I went on the Under 23 tour there, when Romania was still under the Communist rule of Nicolai Ceaucescu. It was my first representative tour. The country was effectively a police state. I remember that whenever we went out, which was not too often, every time we looked over our shoulders there would be a guy in a black leather coat and a trilby about 50 yards behind us, following us around. It was quite an experience being followed around everywhere."

By 1985 Andrew had matured into a very promising fly-half and then it was the Romanians who had to look over their shoulders almost from the start. "I dropped a goal after something like 70 seconds," said Andrew. "It sort of kick-started my international career."

As for his debut as England captain, in Bucharest in May four years later, he admitted: "The match came just after the Lions party to tour Australia had been announced and I was very disappointed not to have been selected. The Romania game and the captaincy therefore came at a good time."

Debutant centre Jeremy Guscott scored a hat-trick of tries, Andrew another drop goal and at the end of that year the Ceaucescu regime was ended in a bloody civil war. By then Andrew, having been called up as a replacement by the Lions, had played a part in the historic series win over the Wallabies.

He is joined in the Wall of Fame by former Romania captain **Mircea Paraschiv**, who led

Not just in it for kicks… England boot boy Rob Andrew

A popular Romanian leader... captain Mircea Paraschiv

the side at Twickenham in 1985. Paraschiv, who won 62 caps at scrum-half for his country had also captained Romania to victory over Wales in 1983, having called the shots in the close-run affair against New Zealand two years previously.

Now both men have a permanent place at Twickenham, as part of a tribute to players from all over the rugby world to mark their achievements in and contribution to the global game.

The last word goes to Andrew. "Ever since my first visit to Twickenham for the 1982 Varsity match the place has been very special. Although there were only perhaps 25,000 people for that game I remember when our captain John Kingston left the tunnel the roar that greeted him was like nothing I had ever experienced. I was still in the bowels of the West stand, second last in the Cambridge queue and I remember thinking, "Christ, what is happening here?"

"There are so many great memories of the place, among them the three Grand Slams which were completed in front of our own supporters and Newcastle's Tetley's Bitter Cup final win. That was extra special for me. But, then, so is the Twickenham experience."

Cyril Towers

Australia Centre

Born: 30.7.1906
Died: 8.6.1985
Caps: 19
Debut: v New Zealand 1926
Last app: v South Africa 1937

Ronald Cove-Smith

England Second row

Born: 26.11.1899
Died: 9.3.1988
Caps: 29
Debut: v Scotland 1921
Last app: v Ireland 1929

It was 59 years after their 1927-28 tour of Britain, Ireland and France, and, sadly, a year after his death, that **Cyril Towers'** Test appearances for Australia moved into double figures.

In 1986 Mr John Dedrick, the then Australian Rugby Union Executive Director, confirmed that the Union had retrospectively granted international Test status to the tour and later matches against New Zealand were also upgraded taking Towers from nine to 19 caps with a couple of strokes of a pen. But at least the ARU did eventually see sense.

The reason for the elevation of the New South Wales Waratahs (as they were known when they toured) was that they were Australia's sole representatives in Rugby Union at that time following the withdrawal of Queensland from the ARU in the 1920s.

Towers, who died in 1985, was regarded as one of the finest centres Australia has ever produced, the pity of it was that he played so few times for Australia. He missed out on the 1933 tour to South Africa after a falling out with an administrator and made just four more appearances between 1934 and 1937.

He is described in one history of Australian Rugby as "… a player without weakness, with a rare blend of fierce aggression and bravado." Apparently though there was one minor flaw in this Antipodean gem. "His sole frailty was that he could only step off his left foot and could not cut back off the right."

No matter. He clearly did enough to warrant posthumous caps and the unstinting praise that preceded the acknowledgement of his 'one frailty', as well as his elevation to the Wall of Fame at Twickenham.

And at least the crowd at Twickenham in 1928 was able to witness Towers as he marked his appearance there – Australia's first official appearance at HQ and only their second Test in all against England – with his first try for his country.

Unfortunately it was not enough to earn victory, that went to England under the captaincy of Towers' co-inductee on to the World Rugby Museum's Wall of Fame at Twickenham, **Ronald Cove-Smith.**

This match on January 7 1928 marked the first of his seven games as captain – the opening six of which England won. Sadly after the seventh, against Ireland the good doctor not only lost the captaincy, he never played for England again. But among those half dozen victories was a Grand Slam in 1928.

In all Cove-Smith, who made his debut in 1921, against Scotland, won 29 caps and also captained the British Isles and Ireland on the tour of South Africa in 1924.

He was a member of England's Grand Slam-winning sides of 1921, 1923 and 1924 as well as that of 1928, when he was the captain.

Cove-Smith had attended Merchant Taylors School in London, before going up to Cambridge where he won rugby Blues in 1919, 1920 and 1921. He captained the Light Blues in his third year, although sadly his only victory in the Varsity match came on his first appearance in 1919.

He played his club rugby for Old Merchant Taylors, naturally, as well as turning out for King's College Hospital.

Cove-Smith became a distinguished physician and at one point in his career was vice president of the British Medical Association.

Ronald Poulton

England Centre

Born: 12.9.1889
Died: 4.5.1915
Caps: 17
Debut: v France 1909
Last app: v France 1914

Jean Prat

France Wing forward

Born: 1.8.1923
Died: 25.2.2005
Caps: 51
Debut: v British Army 1945
Last app: v Italy 1955

The story goes that when France beat England at Twickenham in 1955, their captain, **Jean Prat**, making his last appearance at HQ, took a leaf out of Henry V's book.

There were ten minutes remaining, France were leading, but England were fighting back. Prat, so legend has it, drew his charges around him and, in what was surely one of the game's first huddles, exhorted them: "For centuries you have put up with the bloody English annoying you, surely you can hold them off for another 10 minutes?"

They duly did so, Prat crowning a fine record against England by landing his second drop goal of the match. No wonder the flanker was dubbed 'Monsieur Rugby' by Pat Marshall, the rugby correspondent of the *Daily Express* at that time. And there is little doubt that this gifted ball-player appeared to be able to do it all and some on the rugby field.

This master of all aspects of the game certainly did plenty when France finally broke their duck at Twickenham in 1951 – their 11th visit to HQ – scoring a try, a conversion and a drop goal for an eight-point tally.

In all he was on the winning side against England on five occasions out of a total of nine meetings between the two countries from 1947 to 1955, when he amassed a total of 27 points.

He also had the cheek to land three drop goals, annoying for England since in those days it was hardly *de rigueur* for a flank forward, and a French one at that, to have that sort of ability.

It is, therefore, appropriate that Monsieur Rugby should have been the first Frenchman to be elevated to the Wall of Fame, which is to stand outside the World Rugby Museum at Twickenham.

"I am enchanted and deeply honoured to be the first French player on the wall," he said from his retreat deep in the Pyrenees Mountains above Lourdes. "I have very fond memories of Twickenham. Very fond memories indeed."

M. Rugby had all the ability going. He had an embarrassment of riches; he was a ferocious tackler, quick off the mark, with great hands and a nimble mind and, of course, a wickedly accurate boot on him.

Monsieur Rugby… France's legendary flanker Jean Prat

And no one has forgotten him either. Whenever he goes to watch Lourdes play, however discreetly he tries to lose himself among the crowd, he is always spotted and given VIP treatment.

Age has not withered him. He was always possessed of a powerful personality and trenchant views. His thoughts on the modern-day French side were typically outspoken.

"I am a supporter of France, but I fear for them at Twickenham," he said presciently ahead of their 25-17 defeat at HQ in 2003. "They are not playing good rugby at the moment. It is going to be a terrible game for them. They are just not equipped to deal with England. It is a pity that Thomas Castaignède is injured. He is the best attacking player in France."

He was dismissive of the then France coach Bernard Laporte's strongly held tenet that winning is 90 per cent defence and 10 per cent attack.

"When you are defending you do not have the ball," he said. "And when you do not have the ball you cannot score any points. Of course defence is important, but attacking is what wins games."

Unorthodox and brilliant... England centre Ronnie Poulton

He is joined on the World Rugby Museum's Wall of Fame by **Ronnie Poulton (later Poulton Palmer)**, who was killed by a sniper in fighting at Ploegsteert Wood in May 1915, just 13 months after captaining England to the 1914 Grand Slam, to give the Red Rose Team their first back-to-back Grand Slams.

He had made his England debut after impressing in the 1909 Varsity Match, where he had dominated proceedings, to the extent that this match was thereafter referred to as 'Poulton's Match'.

He ran in five tries in all as Oxford, who had been reduced to 14 men when they lost one of their centres Frank Tarr (who also made his England debut in 1909) with a broken collar bone early in the first half, ran away with victory.

Poulton's first try came after just three minutes and finished off his scoring feat in the second half.

He was an outstanding centre, if an unorthodox one by early Twentieth Century standards, he was always moving around looking for openings and angles, and that made him a tricky man with whom to combine. He also had a remarkable swerve, as well as a deceptive sidestep, which had left defences floundering in his wake since his days at Rugby School, not to mention a peculiar style of running whereby he held the ball in both hands out in front of him.

He did not make quite such a sensational impact for England, although he did score four tries against France to help England clinch the 1914 Grand Slam in style. In all he scored eight tries for England before his playing career was so rudely interrupted by the First World War.

He had by then changed his name by adding Palmer to it after he became the heir to the Huntley and Palmer biscuit empire.

Rory Underwood
England Wing

Born: 19.6.1963
Caps: 85
Debut: v Ireland 1984
Last app: v Ireland 1996

Massimo Giovanelli
Italy Wing forward

Born: 1.3.1967
Caps: 60
Debut: v Zimbabwe 1989
Last app: v Scotland 2000

Rory Underwood may be England's most capped wing, but he acknowledged that sporting heroes are all too readily forgotten once they have retired from their chosen sport.

That is why he greeted his induction to the Wall of Fame at Twickenham with such pride. "It is always good to be recognised for sporting achievement," he said, "and in this case for it to be by the Rugby Football Union makes it even more special.

"Perhaps in America they go a bit over the top with their Halls of Fame, but over here I doubt if there are many people who recall the likes of the great Wales players of the 1970s, other than the Welsh themselves. And that is a shame because youngsters in succeeding generations should be made aware of past sporting heroes."

Underwood remembered his first meeting with Italy in the 1991 World Cup. "We were expected to win," he recalled, "they were an up-and-coming side, but even then they had a couple of fine players. My opposing winger, Paolo Vaccari was a fine player, so was their centre, the late Ivan Francescato.

"Seeing where they are now they are fully deserving of their place in the old Five Nations. They have added another dimension to the tournament."

England won the match 36-6 but Underwood's fellow inductee **Massimo Giovanelli** recalled it for another reason. "When we arrived for the World Cup I think everyone thought that the only thing that came out of Italy was pasta and pizza," said the former Italian flanker of the piratical looks.

"We were accused of dirty play and cheating, but we played a good defensive game. And it was one of my proudest moments to play at Twickenham, which is the Mount Olympus of rugby."

The Parma-born Giovanelli reckoned that Rugby Union was perfectly suited to the gladiatorial nature of the majority of Italian males. Sadly, having enjoyed a piece of history with Italy's opening match in the Six Nations, he was forced to retire after suffering a serious eye injury after winning his 60th cap in the famous victory over Scotland in Rome in 2000.

In full flight… England's sizzling winger Rory Underwood

But he will not be forgotten and has now become a permanent fixture at his 'Mount Olympus'. "It is like a dream to receive this honour," he said of his inclusion on the Wall of Fame.

A gladiator of the game... Italy's hard man Massimo Giovanelli

Sean Fitzpatrick

New Zealand Hooker

Born: 4.6.1963
Caps: 92
Debut: v France 1986
Last app: v Wales 1997

Hal Sever

England Wing

Born: 3.3.1910
Died: 2.6.2005
Caps: 10
Debut: v New Zealand 1936
Last app: v Scotland 1938

Had **Sean Fitzpatrick** been born in the early 20th Century, as was **Hal Sever**, his co-inductee onto the Twickenham Wall of Fame, it is unlikely, however good he was, that the All Black hooker would have amassed as many New Zealand caps.

The brilliance of Fitzpatrick, one of the hardest of competitors, who was graced with superb skills and tremendous athleticism, had marked him out for fame from his debut against France in 1986.

But his total of 92 All Black appearances was another factor which ensured him worldwide immortality in the sport. Pity Sever then.

The Sale wing – only the second player from the club to play for England when he was first capped – made just 10 appearances for England, hardly long enough to etch your name into the history books of the game. Even his big moment, on his debut against the 1936 New Zealand tourists was overshadowed.

It was only the third meeting between the two countries following the tours by the 'Originals' at Crystal Palace in 1905 and the 'Invincibles' at Twickenham in 1925, both of which had ended in victory for the All Blacks.

New Zealand arrived at Twickenham on the back of a defeat by one point against Wales in Cardiff, having disposed quite comfortably of Scotland and Ireland in their opening two tests.

By a quirk of fate the match was also Prince Alexander Obolensky's first appearance for England. Coincidentally he too was a wing, although there the similarities ended. Obolensky was a Russian prince, Sever, while being a member of the privileged classes, was still a commoner.

Perhaps that could explain why Obolensky stole Sever's thunder, it could be that he claimed rugby's equivalent of *droit de seigneur*, which allowed him to score first. In fact he had marked his debut with two scintillating tries before Sever was eventually given a look-in.

But Sever's was no bad score, even if it did not have quite the drama and exhilaration of the pacy Russian's two scores. Centre Peter Cranmer made a break late in the game, found Sever

The complete hooker... the athletic All Black Sean Fitzpatrick

A match-winner... Sale and England wing Hal Sever

and the Sale flier stormed over near the posts for what was to be the first of five tries by him for his country.

It sealed an historic moment for England by helping them to their first victory over the All Blacks – another 37 years were to pass before the All Blacks were beaten by the All Whites again.

Fortunately for Sever his international career lasted longer than Obolensky's, half a dozen matches more to be precise, which was certainly long enough to allow him to make his mark for his country. The following season saw him land a drop goal to help seal victory over Wales at HQ and in the next match against Ireland again at Twickenham came his grandest moment.

There were some five minutes left of the match when, from a scrum, England opted to run the ball from inside their 25. The ball travelled down the line to Sever on the left wing and he scorched down the touchline on an elusive run which left defender after would-be tackler floundering in his wake, before diving over for the match-winning try with an Irishman clinging to his back.

Sever, who attended Shrewsbury School, playing football and cricket there, but not rugby, became an actuary, and was general manager of Refuge Assurance, who backed cricket's 40-over Sunday League for many years.

Sadly Sever died in June 2005, before his induction on to the World Rugby Museum's Wall of Fame. Up to his death he had been the oldest surviving England international. His views of the modern game, professionalism, its entertainment value and of course the modern-day stadium that is Twickenham, would have been fascinating to have known, but the chances are that his feelings about Twickenham are summed up by New Zealand's legendary hooker Fitzpatrick, the son of former All Black five-eighth, the late Brian Fitzpatrick, who died in 2006.

Sean remembered the headquarters of English rugby very fondly. "The first time I played at Twickenham was against the Barbarians in 1989," he recalled recently. "For me it was a great day. To be playing on the ground I had only ever seen on grainy television pictures 12,000 miles away.

"I remember that the grass was very long and it was before all the rebuilding so the old stand was close to the pitch."

His experiences at Twickenham though are mixed. "My next game there was in the 1991 Rugby World Cup. It was against England in a Pool match which we won." But the inaugural winners of the trophy were destined to finish as also-rans after Australia beat England in the final.

By the time of his next visit in November 1993, Fitzpatrick had been promoted to captain of the All Blacks, a role he carried out a record 51 times until his retirement in 1997.

That 1993 match was an ill-fated one though, coming, as it did, ten years after England had last beaten the All Blacks at the same venue. "We lost that one," he said, "and then in 1997 we drew for the first time in the history of the fixture."

But that does not diminish the fondness and admiration in which Fitzpatrick holds the old place. "Nowadays it is a wonderful stadium. The whole set-up is quite extraordinary, it is right up there as one of the great sports stadia in the world. And then there is the singing. There has always been singing at Twickenham, but there is no singing in New Zealand. That is a huge contrast.

"And I think that winning the 2003 Rugby World Cup has helped to create the beginnings of a rugby culture in England." Twickenham is clearly at the heart of it and also in the heart of Fitzpatrick

Richard Sharp

England Outside-half

Born: 9.9.1938
Caps: 14
Debut: v Wales 1960
Last app: v Australia 1967

Sporting immortality – the sort that gave cricket 'Botham's Ashes' in 1981, or football its 'Matthews Cup final' in 1953 – is something few sportsmen achieve in their lifetime.

But in 1963, the coldest winter for 17 years and one that was to become known as The Big Freeze, Rugby Union was able to accord one match to one man.

It was the game which clinched the Five Nations Championship outright for England for the second time in six years.

The setting was Twickenham. Scotland were the opponents. Richard Sharp, the latest inductee on to the World Rugby Museum's Wall of Fame, was 'The Man.'

And it is perfectly understandable why this Calcutta Cup of all Calcutta Cups was dubbed 'Richard Sharp's match' because his contribution was little short of stunning. Not just because of his own natural brilliance, but because it was the start of the big thaw, when winter began to lose its icy grip on the country, and Spring poked through the coating of ice and snow. Sharp's contribution on the afternoon of Saturday March 16 1963 sent a warm glow through the whole of game and melted even the hardest of hearts.

But to appreciate England's, and Sharp's, achievement it is necessary to start with the first snowfall of the year. Those first flakes fell on Boxing Day night and the world was to remain imprisoned in an unyielding white mantle until the end of March. That vicious cold spell embraced the Five Nations Championship, when pitches were so hard that straw was spread over them to try to render them a little more conducive to rugby.

Sharp was appointed captain for the Championship. "It was a huge honour to be appointed captain of my country," he said. "I did my best, but I had a very good side, with the likes of Mike Weston, Malcolm Phillips and of course at scrum-half Dickie Jeeps. I loved playing outside him, he was a wonderful player."

England's campaign was to begin at Cardiff Arms Park. The run-up to the match had been marked by severe blizzards and conditions were, at best, Arctic.

That of course affected both teams' build-up to the match. Sharp recalled England's preparations, which had an ironic look to them, since they all had to repair to the seaside, despite it being mid-winter, because no suitable pitches could be found on which to train.

"It was that very cold year, when the grounds were all frozen. It had been so cold that the final England trial, which should have been played at Twickenham, had to be played in Torquay, where it was milder.

"Then we went over to Wales. Traditionally the England team used to stay in Porthcawl and we would train on Porthcawl Rugby Club's ground, but the pitch there was so frozen that we had to train on the beach. It shows just how professional the game is today, because before an international we had a run around on a beach."

But whether it was the sand, or the bracing Bristol Channel air at Porthcawl, something was right, because a sure-footed Red Rose team triumphed at the Arms Park, the last side to win there until Will Carling's Grand Slam team in 1991, although there had been a draw in 1983. Sharp reckoned England were lucky to come away from Cardiff with victory though. "We were fortunate to win," said Sharp.

"We could so easily have lost. We were up against a very good Wales side and early on one of the Wales wingers, I forget which, was through, but he slipped on the ice, if he hadn't he would have scored."

It was a callow Wales side in fact, featuring no fewer than five debutants, including the brilliant halfback combo of captain and scrum-half Clive Rowlands and outside half David Watkins. The most experienced player was Swansea flier Dewi Bebb on the left wing.

England's backs were far more experienced, but six of the pack were winning their first cap. Sharp converted England's two tries, scored by Malcolm Phillips, the Fylde centre, and debutant lock John Owen of Coventry. Sharp also landed a drop goal, the third and final one of his career. So England had launched their Championship campaign in positive fashion.

Next up was Ireland, a match which ended in a stultifying – and these days practically unheard of – 0-0 draw. "This time the weather wasn't icy," said Sharp, "It was wet and muddy. The Irish forwards were immensely strong, Bill Mulcahy was their captain, I had been on the Lions tour of South Africa with him the previous year, and he was partnered in the second row by Willie John McBride. They missed a couple of kicks at goal and again I think we were a bit lucky to come away with something."

The draw of course meant that a chance of the Triple Crown had gone, but Sharp's England were still unbeaten, an important factor to take with them into their next match, which was against a formidable France side, at Twickenham.

"The one team we found hardest to beat was France," said Sharp. "In those days pitches were more often than not, muddy, but the French forwards were very quick and very mobile, and they were very effective with their hands. They always seemed to be able to find their backs as well, the forwards' distribution was very good. The French games were always the toughest ones in those days. So in 1963 we knew we had to keep it tight against France."

And tight was the word to describe the way England handled the French. The forwards controlled the game efficiently, denying France any decent possession. They still let in Guy

Boniface, the outside centre for the only try of the game, but ultimately that did not matter, two penalties by John Willcox ensured the closest of victories for England and kept them on course for the title.

So finally to THE match. The title decider. The Calcutta Cup. The oldest of enemies, England and Scotland, in a head-to-head that proved more effective in the cold spring than any coke-filled brazier for warming up the watchers. This was Sharp's match.

The Scots had arrived a point behind England in the Championship table. Victory for them would give them their first title for 15 years, and they turned up at Twickenham with ferocious intent.

Under the Spring sunshine the Scots began at a heck of a pace with the back row driving hard at the English and the blindside flanker Ronald Glasgow caught a long throw at a line-out and was driven over under a mound of bodies for a try. From a scrum Ken Scotland landed a drop goal and suddenly England, 8-0 down, were up against it.

England hit back shortly before the interval when Peter Jackson combined brilliantly with Sharp (of course) from a line-out, the winger slipping around several defenders before kicking ahead for the forwards to converge on the ball, and eventually prop Nick Drake-Lee was driven over for a try which Willcox converted.

And there was more to follow, because England, and specifically the captain Sharp, had a little something tucked up their sleeve. Sharp explained: "The game has changed of course since our day, but in those days we found it was quite difficult to make breaks and score tries from set scrums. We used to like line-out ball, but at the set pieces the defences were very difficult to break down.

"So we devised a variation at the set scrum, because orthodox movements were not very rewarding."

The set scrum was some 40 yards out from the Scottish line and close to touch. Contemporary reports suggest that a blind-side move was on the cards with right winger Peter Jackson standing close to the scrum-half Simon Clarke.

But in fact the Cambridge Blue halfback opted for an orthodox pass off his right hand to his fly-half Sharp, who continued: "The try that I scored was really thanks to Mike Weston. We arranged a scissors move, whereby the fly-half gets the ball from the scrum-half, I then ran flat across the pitch, Mike came in behind me.

"At that point the fly-half had a choice, either he completed the scissor movement by giving the ball to the man running in the counter direction to the fly-half, or dummying it.

"We hadn't decided which we would do, we set up the scissors and I decided to dummy it, so he rather caused the defence to hesitate, it wasn't blocking or anything, there was nothing illegal about it, it was just a genuine dummy scissors. And because the defence hesitated I was able to go through the gap that it had created."

That got Sharp past the Scotland flanker Kenneth Ross. A quick burst of acceleration and another dummy took Sharp between the bewildered centres David White and Brian Henderson. He was almost there, he just had to get around the fullback Colin Blaikie.

The eye witness accounts state that Sharp sold the hapless Blaikie an outrageous dummy, but Sharp did not see it quite like that.

Sharp had the England left winger Jim Roberts coming up on his left shoulder and a pass outside would have put the Sale threequarter through and over for the winning try. Sharp said: "I remember afterwards that people who perhaps did not know the game so well, saying I had been selfish in dummying the fullback.

"But I didn't really have much choice. I was on the point of passing to Jim so that he could score when I spotted Blaikie just beginning to drift across and I could see he was going to go for Jim, this was even before I had passed the ball. And so I decided not to pass, but went through with the dummy instead, because the decision had effectively been made for me."

The try not only clinched the match, but it sealed the Championship. Twickenham erupted. "It was very pleasing to have scored the winning try," added Sharp, who then dwelt on the atmosphere at Headquarters. "It was an intimate ground. When I was fortunate enough to win my first cap – Bev Risman pulled a hamstring at the last minute so I stepped in – the thing that struck me about a packed Twickenham on an international match day was the noise.

"I had played there before for Oxford University in the Varsity Match and for the Royal Navy in the Inter-Services Tournament, but running out on to the Twickenham pitch for a big international, you suddenly realised how deafening the noise from the crowd is.

"You just heard a roar, and I quickly realised in that first international against Wales that Dickie Jeeps, my captain and scrum-half, and I needed visual signals to communicate with each other. So we devised a simple system of hand signals to tell us what we were intending to do and where we were going."

In his seven Five Nations Championship matches at Twickenham Sharp, who scored 26 points for England when a try was worth three points, was never on the losing side, enjoying five victories and two draws. His 14th and final appearance at headquarters was for England against Australia, in 1967, four years after his 13th cap, and it was a match which ended in defeat, but in those early years of the sixties Twickenham was England's fortress.

Now it is also the place where Sharp's exploits are being commemorated on the World Rugby Museum's Wall of Fame. "I feel hugely honoured," said Sharp, modest to the last. "It is a wonderful honour to have been accorded." The Wall of Fame represents a further rung up the ladder of rugby immortality for one of the game's true greats.

Roger Uttley

England Second row/back row
Born: 11.9.1949
Caps: 23
Debut: v Ireland 1973
Last app: v Scotland 1980

Jean-Pierre Rives

France Wing forward
Born: 31.12.1952
Caps: 59
Debut: v England 1975
Last app: v Scotland 1984

Remarkable as it may seem it was not his first appearance as an England player at Twickenham that **Roger Uttley** remembered clearly, even though victory that day was England's first in the Championship for two years.

Rather it was the England v France fixture two years previously which is etched in his memory. "Gosforth had played Richmond in the morning and then we all went to Twickenham to watch the international in the afternoon," recalled Uttley.

"We were in the old North Stand, surrounded by French fans waving replica cockerels on poles. The atmosphere was fantastic. And the match ended in a draw."

Two years later he was back at headquarters as a player, having won his first cap in the defeat against Ireland a fortnight earlier. "It was a scary prospect," he said. "It was the old Twickenham so the crowd was right on top of us and France were fielding some legendary players, the likes of Lux, Trillo and in the pack Walter Spanghéro, whose very name commanded respect. It was a great occasion." And like so many big occasions it passed in a blur, it must have because Uttley did not remember that England actually won the match.

But he had near-perfect recall of his debut as England captain, again at Twickenham, but this time against Scotland. "I really enjoyed captaining England, there was honour and pride in doing it." He also scored a try – his second and last for his country- late in the game and said: "It was from close range, I just concentrated on keeping my legs pumping and just driving. I went over the line under a pile of bodies, but one of my legs was free and I waved it in celebration at scoring. I was pretty chuffed."

There had been no celebration two years prior to that when Uttley was playing in the second row and his fellow inductee **Jean-Pierre Rives** made his debut on the flank – one of three new caps for France.

Although not scoring himself, Rives, the blond bombshell of a flanker, made enough of a nuisance of himself to suggest what was to follow in the years ahead – an outstanding 59-cap career – and France won a high scoring match 27-20.

Back row man on the frontline... England's Roger Uttley

The all-action Rives, with his long blond hair, was the embodiment of a free spirit in the game; he was totally committed, utterly dedicated, and as ferocious a flanker as you could ever meet; he also possessed a great deal of skill and his 'groundwork' used to produce a great deal of possession for his team-mates. He contributed hugely to what is commonly referred to as 'French flair'.

There were those who had it that the Toulouse-born flanker was too small at 5ft 11in to play at international level, but France's own JPR, quickly gave the lie to that thought.

His career, which saw him captain his country in 34 tests, embraced Grand Slams in 1977 and 1981 as well as a famous victory over the New Zealand All Blacks in Auckland in 1979.

In the early 1990s Rives took up serious sculpture and has exhibited in Europe and the United States of America.

The playing days are often a blur to the men in the centre of the action, but Uttley has better recall of his post-playing career. He distinctly remembered the occasion, when, after the 1991

Blond bomber... France's own JPR, Jean-Pierre Rives

Rugby World Cup final, Uttley, by now the England coach, watched as the late Sir Peter Yarranton, the then President of the RFU, ushered Prime Minister John Major into the steamy home dressing room.

"As they walked in, England flanker Micky Skinner emerged, stark naked from the showers. 'Oh,' said Mick the Munch, 'Prime Minister – top man!'"

Which aptly sums up the calibre of these two inductees on to the World Rugby Museum's Wall of Fame, Rives and Uttley – Top men.

Peter Wheeler

England Hooker

Born: 26.11.1948
Caps: 41
Debut: v France 1975
Last app: v Wales 1984

Mark Ella

Australia Outside-half

Born: 5.6.1959
Caps: 25
Debut: v New Zealand 1980
Last app: v Scotland 1984

Peter Wheeler had only hazy memories of England's thrilling win over the Wallabies on a chill January day at Twickenham in 1982.

The Australians were bristling with talented players, Simon Poidevin, Mark Loane, Brendan Moon, and Wheeler's fellow inductee on to the Wall of Fame, the brilliant Wallaby fly-half **Mark Ella**.

But the name on Wheelbrace's lips when asked what he recalled of the match was that of Erica Roe. Her unscheduled appearance on the hallowed Twickenham turf at half-time turned heads in spectacular fashion, the gaze of pretty well every red-blooded male was drawn to her toplessness. Wheeler and just about every member of the England team were no exception.

Wheeler recalled: "The memories of that day have flowered through multiple telling of this at dinners, and it seems to change a little with each telling to make the story better. Anyway Billy [Beaumont] was captain and at half time I think we were only just ahead, when we had expected to be doing better than we were.

"In those days you didn't go off at half time, you stayed on the pitch and, at Twickenham, you enjoyed your slices of orange and *lemon*. Twickenham was the only ground where you had lemons at half-time, as well as the traditional oranges.

"Anyway, we were listening to Billy in full rant at us about the line-out, when we suddenly became aware that something else was happening on the pitch. There was a load of noise from the spectators. Bill started to get angry and said, 'Come on, we've got an international here.' Then he looked around and saw Erica Roe.

"At this point, when I am telling this tale at a dinner, I maintain it was Smithy [scrum-half Steve Smith] who made this remark, but he maintains it was me. But for the purpose of this interview we shall say it was Smithy. What he said was: 'Hey Bill, there's a bird over there with your bum on her chest.'"

But Wheeler then broke off to reveal that Erica Roe was not the only person to enter the rugby arena that day. "The little known fact about that day is this, it was the era for people running on to the pitch, and while Erica Roe was doing her thing at one end of the Twickenham

Fantastic highs and Erica Row... happy England hooker Peter Wheeler

pitch, at the other end there was a bloke who ran on dressed in a gorilla outfit. It was obviously his big moment. Unfortunately he chose exactly the wrong time to do it, because everyone was watching Erica – or so I thought."

Incredibly, after the match Wheeler discovered that at least one member of the England team, the second row forward Maurice Colclough, had somehow missed seeing Erica, although he had seen the secondary pitch invasion [in fact as revealed earlier, Peter Winterbottom admitted to having seen only the gorilla]. "When we were back in the dressing room after the match I remember I was having a shower and Maurice Colclough came over and said to me, 'I couldn't understand it, there we were in the middle of an international, and all the blokes were getting excited about some bloke dressed up in a gorilla outfit!'"

Wheeler certainly had cause to remember the touring Australians, because he had captained the Midlands in their opening match the previous October at Leicester, home of Wheeler's club the Tigers, and the Midlands won that game.

"In those days Australia were still developing," Wheeler explained. "It wasn't until the early 1990s that they really got going. In fact there's an Irish forward who said that in those days Australia were the sort of team you played three or four times in your career, and you beat them nine times out of ten. That sums them up. They were improving all the time."

In those days touring teams came close to being immigrants, so long did they spend in the British Isles. On that particular tour, which ran from October 1981 to January 1982, the Wallabies played all four home nations, beating Ireland, before going on to lose to Wales, Scotland and, of course, England.

Wheeler lamented the disappearance of prolonged tours in the age of professionalism. "What you don't see now is the touring sides travelling around the country playing against the Midlands, the North, the South West etc. They used to be very special occasions."

There were also more opportunities for club players to get to play at Twickenham back then, as Wheeler explained: "In the amateur era we used to go to Twickenham quite a lot, apart from club games against Harlequins, there would be the final England trial Probables v Possibles, and England versus The Rest.

"There have been some fantastic highs at Twickenham for me. Winning international matches, beating New Zealand, France and Wales, at that time those were massive wins, because they were the biggest challenges you faced in your playing career; the cup finals; victory at Twickenham always had a great impact on you."

Post match was also less frenetic, with no media demands for endless interviews as there are these days, no compulsory appearances in this or that corporate hospitality suite, in those far off days the players were allowed to unwind.

"One of the nice things I used to like as a player about Twickenham in those days, when you have been away from your family for a few days [preparing for the match], was that after a game you would go into the West Car Park and have a really nice hour with family and friends.

"Of course that was in the days of the old Twickenham, which always had a great atmosphere, the stands were so close to the pitch."

A man who made his mark... the hugely gifted Wallaby fly-half Mark Ella

Not that the new stadium has lost any of its magic for the modern-day player. Wheeler insisted: "There is a lot of tradition and history with Twickenham, and modern-day players respect that. Going to Twickenham means something to them as well.

But perhaps one or two of the amateur traditions have disappeared. "Apart from the lemons at half-time there were other things that were peculiar to Twickenham in my day. For example we would come out on to the pitch for a team photograph about half an hour before the kick-off. That was good because you can look back on those photos every now again and recall team-mates who were there, and bring up memories of that and other games.

"Then when you went back into the dressing room the president of the RFU would come in accompanied by one or two members of the committee to wish us good luck."

As with practically every inductee on to the World Rugby Museum's Wall of Fame, Wheeler also had fond memories of the facilities. "The dressing rooms were huge, compared with the normal club facilities. They covered a vast area."

In all Wheeler won 41 caps for his country, captaining them in five Tests and leading them to victory on two occasions. He had made his captaincy debut in a non-cap match against Canada in 1983. It was in that same year that Wheeler got his first taste of Test captaincy, something of a baptism of fire since it was against a formidable All Blacks team. "That was in the November, my 37th cap," he recalled, "and we won 15-9. Colclough scored a try for us. I remember that match a little better than the win over Australia, because you don't beat the All Blacks all that often in your career. That was obviously a special moment."

He also led Leicester to three successive John Player Cup triumphs at HQ. "When, in 1979, we won the inaugural John Player Cup, that was memorable, because it was done with my clubmates. It's special winning something with your club because week-in week-out you are training with the guys and playing together.

Wheeler joins a prestigious group of rugby legends from all over the world. His co-inductee Mark Ella, twin of another Wallaby international Glen, and older brother of centre Gary, who, like Glen made just four appearances for Australia, was a relatively raw outside half when he and Wheeler crossed paths in 1982. But Erica Roe would certainly have made his sixth appearance memorable.

He had not begun the tour as the first choice No10, Paul McLean was regarded as being a steadier option, and with a reliable boot, and he appeared against Ireland and Wales, but halfway through the programme the Wallaby coach Bob Templeton opted for the less predictable, more exciting Ella, who faced Scotland and England.

Ella, who captained his country on four occasions, retired from the game prematurely at 25, but in that short time he had established himself as one of the finest fly-halves in the world.

His rugby intellect was MENSA standard, his instincts unmatched by any contemporary. He thrilled crowds with his reading of a game and his ability to draw defenders before unleashing the talented Wallaby backs into the space just created.

In all Ella won 25 caps – many feel it could, and should, have been four times that number – and while his first taste of Twickenham as a full-blown Wallaby ended in defeat, he enjoyed something of a personal triumph on his return to the ground two years later, when he scored a try in Australia's comprehensive 19-3 victory over England. That Wallaby line-up included two players who were eventually to become legends in their own right, it was Michael Lynagh's second cap (he played in the centre) and scrum-half Nick Farr-Jones's debut.

It was on that 1984 tour that Ella became the first player to score a try in each of the four internationals, a personal Grand Slam of sorts.

But Ella also enjoys legendary status in the rugby world for some of the wonderful touches he displayed. He was a flair player, an exciting player, someone who could turn a match in an instant. He certainly graced the Twickenham stage with his talent, as did the characterful Wheeler, and both deserve this signal honour from the World Rugby Museum.

Will Carling

England Centre

Born: 12.12.1965
Caps: 72
Debut: v France 1988
Last app: v Wales 1997

Hugo Porta

Argentina Outside-half

Born: 11.9.1951
Caps: 60
Debut: v Chile 1971
Last app: v World XV 1999

The match was over. The crowd was dispersing. The stadium echoed to the occasional call of a triumphant supporter, or the slap and bang of cables as technicians dismantled the tons of broadcasting paraphernalia which winds itself around big sporting events.

Then out of the now-darkened tunnel a shadowy figure emerged and stepped onto the hallowed turf of HQ.

He moved out towards the middle of the pitch, echoes of past triumphs reverberating in his memory; matches won, matches lost; tries scored, heroes made; tears of joy, weeping in defeat.

"Oi! You! What do you think you're doing? Get off the pitch, now!" The indignant member of the Twickenham groundstaff reinforced his instruction by making his way urgently towards the chunky, powerful figure who was still half concealed in the gloom.

Then he stopped, recognising the man in front of him. "Oh, it's you Will. Oh, that's all right, stay out here as long as you like."

It is a bizarre, yet touching memory to have of the ground where, as captain of England, **Will Carling** had led his team to back-to-back Grand Slams – the first Englishman ever to do so; each one was concluded at Twickenham.

He had also played in a World Cup final on his home turf in 1991 and limped out of his leadership in March 1996 after the fickle turf caught his studs and he had to be carried off after 32 minutes of his final match as captain.

"I do have other memories of Twickenham, of course," he added. "The two Grand Slams which were both settled at the ground, beating New Zealand in 1993 is another. That was special. But there are so many. Too many. Most of them good."

His first match as captain of England in 1988 set a fairly high standard, victory over the much-vaunted Wallabies. The choice of Carling as captain by England manager Geoff Cooke had been questioned hotly, many feeling that the Harlequin, a former Army officer, was too young at 22. But Carling rose above it and proved to be an able and at times a charismatic leader.

Captain Marvel... Will Carling led England to three Grand Slams

Under him England rose to great heights, with a string of famous victories and a stack of achievements.

He should now have one more memory to add to the list. Carling remains one of the most successful captains in modern-day rugby union history, having led his team to victory 44 times in 59 matches at the helm; that gives him a 74.58 percentage of success.

His achievements in the game are legion so it is no surprise that he has been elevated to the Wall of Fame.

"I am amazed," said Carling, who was joined on the World Rugby Museum's Wall of Fame by **Hugo Porta**, the legendary Argentinian fly-half. "It never occurred to me that anyone would ever think of me in such terms. I am deeply honoured."

Yet he regards his fellow inductee Porta in pretty much the same terms. "When I was younger I watched him and I thought then what a great player he was," said Carling.

"To have had such an influence on the game when playing for a country that was still in a developmental phase is extraordinary. Few, if any, players have commanded the same respect from their peers when playing for one of the lesser sides.

A well-respected man… Argentina's fly-half Hugo Porta

"And as a man he displays dignity and there is a charm about him. He was as good a fly-half as there has ever been in world rugby." Carling was not such a bad player either.

However much Carling did for England in the run-up to professionalism, then, it has to be said, Porta did even more for Argentina.

When he made his debut in 1971 the Pumas were not in the frame where world rugby was concerned, but by the time of his retirement two decades later Argentina were firmly on the World Rugby map.

Porta amassed 592 points for Argentina, although in his one appearance at Twickenham in 1990, the man with one of the deadliest boots in the world game, failed to score a single point as Los Pumas slumped to a 51-0 defeat.

These days Porta, among other things, is occupied with trying to convert the Tri-Nations into a quadrangular tournament by installing Argentina as the fourth side, joining Australia, New Zealand and South Africa.

Lewis Jones

Wales Fullback

Born: 11.4.1931
Caps: 10
Debut: v England 1950
Last app: v France 1952

JPR Williams

Wales Fullback

Born: 2.3.1949
Caps: 55
Debut: v Scotland 1969
Last app: v Scotland 1981

Two Wales' fullbacks join other rugby legends on Twickenham's World Rugby Museum's Wall of Fame. **JPR Williams** took England apart with two tries in 1976, when Wales went on to complete their second Grand Slam of the 70s.

He shared in another Grand Slam two years later in 1978 and contributed mightily to other Wales' successes as well as to the British and Irish Lions, for whom he made eight appearances.

Williams had by then established himself as a legend. He was known by his initials, JPR, and also for his mutton-chop sideburns and the bandana which held his longish hair in place during matches; but he was known also for the way he played the game, which was fearlessly, thrillingly and skilfully, whether it was for Wales, the British and Irish Lions, London Welsh or Bridgend. His incursions into the line were to be feared because his appearance among the threequarters invariably spelled trouble for the opposition, because JPR's instincts for scoring were so sharply honed, he attacked with prescience and precision.

He was renowned for his courage – most famously returning to the fray after a stamp by the All Blacks John Ashworth left him with an injury which required 30 stitches, but once they had been inserted he returned to the fray – his deadly counter-attacking, as well as his magnificent defence and wonderful footballing skills, marked him out as one of the finest fullbacks in the world.

He liked Twickenham. He had scored tries there against England before and by the time of that double there was no doubt that he knew precisely where the try-line was at each end of the ground, as well as knowing, of course, where the ground itself was.

But 26 years earlier **Lewis Jones**, Williams' co-inductee on to the World Rugby Museum's Wall of Fame, had no idea where HQ was. Back in 1950 the callow Jones was an 18-year-old conscript in the Royal Navy and had been plucked from the relative obscurity of Devonport Services by the Welsh selectors following the unexpected retirement of Frank Trott.

"Cliff Morgan reminded me recently of the letter we received from the selectors," recalled Jones, who still boasted an impressive golf handicap of 12 in his mid-70s.

"It read something like this, 'You have been selected for Wales versus England at Twickenham

Brave, bold and brilliant… Wales legendary fullback JPR Williams

on 21st January 1950, would you make sure you are at the ground two hours before the kick-off. Shirts, shorts and socks will be supplied. Shorts and socks must be returned after the match.'"

So on the appointed day Jones, on leave from the Navy, set off from Swansea railway station. "I had never been to London before and I had no idea where Twickenham was.

"The train was packed with thousands of Wales supporters and when we arrived in Paddington I decided that all I needed to do was go with the crowds to Twickenham. No one recognised me because I was playing my rugby in the West Country, and I was only a kid of 18, so no one had heard of me.

"I think the selectors were in a quandary at the time. I hadn't even played fullback, I played in the centre. Why they picked me I don't know. I really was extremely lucky to get into the side in the first place. I remember thinking before the trial that I had to find a way to impress them, so I worked out that as a fullback they would need someone who could kick well.

"I decided to kick to the left hand touch with my right foot and to the right hand touch with my left, even though I could not kick well with my left foot. I managed that so the selectors obviously thought 'Here's a lad who kicks with either foot'.

"The selectors would also be looking for a fullback who could tackle, which was not my strong suit. But Windsor Major presented me with the simplest of tackles when he sprinted down the wing. I tackled him into touch and I think the selectors believed that they had discovered a great tackling fullback. In fact what I really had to offer them was my speed."

He may have arrived at Twickenham as an unknown, but by 5pm that day the name Lewis Jones was on the lips of all 75,500 supporters who had witnessed Wales' first victory at Twickenham since 1933 and only their second at HQ.

"I only remember a couple of things about the match," said Jones, from his home in Leeds. "The first was when I ran across the pitch and managed to tackle John Smith, the England wing, into the corner flag, on the right hand side at the South Stand end."

The second was a touch of genius by Jones just before half time which turned the match on its head, with England leading at the time.

"I caught the ball in my own 25 and thought about kicking for touch, but there was a gap so I went for it, all the time reminding myself that if I was closed down I could always kick for touch because in those days there were no restrictions about kicking outside your 25.

"As it turned out I didn't have to kick because the England team just parted ahead of me and suddenly I realised I had reached their 25. I had covered 50 yards untouched. I found support and a couple of passes later the prop Cliff Davies scored a try. At the end of the match the crowd was allowed on to the pitch and I was carried off on their shoulders."

Jones converted Wales' second try scored by Ray Cale and also landed a penalty to secure the first win of what was to become the Red Dragons' first Triple Crown for 39 years.

Shortly after winning his tenth Wales cap he left Rugby Union, having played at fullback, on the wing and once in his preferred position of centre. Jones joined Leeds Rugby League club for £6,000 – "It took me a year to spend it all, because that was a lot of money in those days." – where he became a legend, captaining the club to the first Championship success in their history. He went on to play 15 times for Great Britain, which makes him quite a rare bird in that he had also played for the British and Irish Lions in his annus mirabilis.

"That year, 1950, was wonderful. When George Norton, the Ireland fullback, broke his arm I was called up to replace him."

The Lions had sailed to New Zealand, but there was no time for Jones to make a leisurely voyage. He was flown to the Land of the Long White Cloud, the first player ever to be flown out to a tour.

"When I arrived at London Airport I looked out at the plane, it was a monster. A Boeing Stratocruiser. No doubt by today's standards it would be dwarfed by the Jumbos and so on, but to me it was huge."

Jones' flight followed the Pacific route, flying out to Los Angeles then south over the Pacific ocean, a journey which in these days means 24 hours flying time to New Zealand. Back then it was somewhat different.

"It took four and a half days, with four or five changes of planes to fly there. We landed in Gisburn on the east coast and my first game was the following day."

But it was clearly a memorable trip, recalled with clarity and fondness by Jones, who went into teaching after his Rugby playing days were over. Oddly, although he has been inducted into the Wales Hall of Fame he has yet to have any similar recognition from Rugby League. Perhaps that will change now that the World Rugby Museum at Twickenham has honoured him.

Willie John McBride

Ireland Second row

Born: 6.6.1940
Caps: 63
Debut: v England 1962
Last app: v Wales 1975

Simon Geoghegan

Ireland Wing

Born: 1.9.1968
Caps: 37
Debut: v France 1991
Last app: v England 1996

Two Irishman have been inducted on to the World Rugby Museum's Wall of Fame courtesy of their exploits at Twickenham, **Willie John McBride** and **Simon Geoghegan**.

Of the two, it is the former, McBride who can truly be described as a Colossus of Rugby Union, a living legend.

He bestrode the game as a formidable second row forward through the 60s and well into the 70s, and will forever be remembered for the infamous '99' call when captaining the British and Irish Lions in South Africa in 1974.

That call signalled mayhem as the Lions got their retaliation in first against a physical Springboks team – "We were bullied at times over there, so we finally stood up for ourselves," he explained.

But McBride did so much more in Rugby Union than shout out a coded call to arms in South Africa. Twickenham was one of many placed where he made his mark.

"I have quite a history at Twickenham," said McBride, who made a record 17 Test appearances for the Lions as well as 63 for Ireland – at one stage he was the world's most capped lock thanks to those 80 tests. "And not a bad record either."

McBride made his Ireland debut at headquarters in 1962. "I always found Twickenham a most hospitable place to be through all my years as a player. And to be inducted on to the World Rugby Museum's Wall of Fame is a great honour.

"I came into the game relatively late though, I was 17 when I took it up and four years later I was trotting out at Twickenham for my first Ireland cap."

Unfortunately it was not a winning start to his career, England won that match, the first of McBride's 14 games against the Red Rose team, 16-0.

"Prior to my Ireland debut I had played in front of the proverbial one man and his dog, but when I went out on the Twickenham pitch I could not believe what I saw. There were all these people, it was bloody frightening."

The losing start to his distinguished international career which spanned 14 years, did not

Yer Man... Ireland's and the Lions legend Willie John McBride

prevent the selectors from picking McBride for the British and Irish Lions tour to South Africa in the summer of 1962.

"You don't forget your first cap for your country, there is nothing like it," added McBride, "it is that sort of thing that sticks in your mind for the rest of your life.

"Even though we lost I decided afterwards that I could only get better. If I remember rightly that was the game in which the England fly-half Richard Sharp had a great game.

"And after the match was over and we had been well beaten there was the consolation of those baths. I had never seen anything like it. They were all ready and filled with steaming water as we came into the dressing room. It was lovely just sinking in to the water."

Light on his feet... the slick and slippery Ireland wing Simon Geoghegan

But that is not the only memory of luxury that McBride harbours. He called to mind the match at headquarters eight years later, in 1970, when the Ireland selectors recalled Tony O'Reilly, the wing, after a seven year absence on the international scene.

Like other of his Ireland team-mates he remembered the arrival in a chauffeur-driven limousine. "He was already a very successful businessman by then and he even got the chauffeur to carry his kit into the changing room. He loved all that nonsense.

"On the day of the match the weather was horrible, the Twickenham pitch was a mess and O'Reilly? I wouldn't say he played on the wing, he was on the wing would be more accurate. The conditions did not suit him.

"I think he played his best rugby for the Lions, particularly against New Zealand, when he had all those good backs inside him. But he was a hell of a finisher and in those days he was big for a winger. He was a big man, well over six feet tall."

But no one came bigger than McBride in Irish Rugby lore, he is a latter day Ulster chieftain, a Cuchulainn of the modern world.

After all the talk of Dr Sir Tony O'Reilly, more recently Ireland had another winger who made quite an impact at Twickenham. In fact **Simon Geoghegan**, McBride's co-inductee on to the World Rugby Museum's Wall of Fame, had a hand, and both feet, in England's downfall in 1994. It was a famous Ireland victory since no one had beaten England at Twickenham since Wales in 1988 – oddly it was a winger on that day, two-try Adrian Hadley, who did for the Red Rose on that occasion.

If you listen to the solicitor, Geoghegan, whose rugby career was ended prematurely by a chronic toe injury leaving him with 37 Ireland caps, he will tell you that he did just two things in that game.

"In those days as a winger," said Geoghegan, "you might get one pass in five matches and then you were expected to be able to do something, rounding a half dozen defenders to score a try."

He actually had more touches than that, though. When Ireland won a scrum Michael Bradley flung the ball out, fullback Conor O'Shea and centre Maurice Field set off on dummy runs and with the white line thus stretched, the ball found its way to Geoghegan out on the left.

He scorched outside Tony Underwood, then fixed England fullback Jon Callard to cross for a wonderful try.

The odd thing was, with so many Bath players in the England squad, that no one picked up on the move. As Geoghegan explained: "Bath had pulled that move on us at London Irish a couple of seasons earlier.

"George Hook was our coach at Irish at the time and we worked on it and developed it a little. Then, because of George's involvement with Ireland at that time, the national side also practised it. And when we put it into practice it came off."

Geoghegan's try and Eric Elwood's conversion nosed Irish ahead by a point, but then came the clincher. Geoghegan gathered a Callard chip, shimmied and swerved his way through the chasing Englishmen before launching a kick some 40 metres upfield.

With his electric pace the Ireland winger arrived at the ball a split second after Rob Andrew had fallen on it. Geoghegan dived on to the England fly-half and tussled for possession and French referee Patric Thomas awarded Ireland a penalty after deeming that Andrew should have released the ball. Elwood's kick and Ireland's subsequent tenacious defence ensured that England were denied victory.

But Geoghegan was big enough to admit that the referee got it wrong. "It should have been a penalty to England," said the former London Irish and Bath player.

"I did not stay on my feet and I should have been penalised for that." He wasn't, and the rest is history.

And at least it meant Geoghegan, born in Barnet, in North London, but a proud Irishman for all that, had enjoyed what was in those days a rare thing – a victory over England, and on their home turf to boot, no mean feat.

Geoghegan was fond of the Twickenham of those days. "I have been to the new stadium and it is a great place, but I think there was a better atmosphere in the old stadium.

"The crowd was a lot closer to the pitch. It was a bit like Lansdowne Road, where, when you were pushed into touch you could pick individual faces in the crowd and I remember an

Ireland-England match, it was 1993, when I pulled off one of Brian Moore's boots and threw it into the crowd and they would not give it back straightaway. I remember him remonstrating with them. It did come back to him eventually."

But Twickenham, ancient or modern, will always be special according to Geoghegan. "It was always a hard place for visiting sides to play, but it is great to be able to say you have played there."

And as for his induction on to the World Rugby Museum's Wall of Fame, Geoghegan is unequivocal in his view. "It is a great honour."

Clive Woodward

England Centre

Born: 6.1.1956
Caps: 21
Debut: v Ireland 1980
Last app: v Wales 1984

George Nepia

New Zealand Fullback

Born: 25.4.1905
Died: 27.8.1986
Caps: 9
Debut: v Ireland 1924
Last app: v British and
Irish Lions 1930

It would not be unreasonable to expect that the greatest memory of Twickenham would be a player's international debut at HQ where the roar of the Elliman's Rub and the smell of the crowd would be stamped, indelibly, on the eye and the mind.

But that conventional backtrack does not quite work for **Clive Woodward**. His best memory of Twickenham 'The Place', as opposed to Twickenham 'The Occasion' comes some half a dozen years before he made his international debut.

"It was the September, before I went up to Loughborough," recalled Woodward, the former England manager. "I was playing for Harlequins and I remember we had a match against Cardiff. In those days Quins played all their big games over the road from The Stoop Memorial Ground, at Twickenham.

"I was 18. It was my first visit to Twickenham and here I was in the same team as the great England fullback Bob Hiller and on the opposite side among a clutch of internationals was Gareth Edwards.

"There were three men and a dog to watch the game, but that did not matter to me because here I was using the same changing rooms that were used for internationals and on the same pitch with some great Test players. It was an amazing feeling and a great experience. It was great to get an opportunity to play there with the club."

Thereafter the memories of his England appearances there rather blurred – all ten of them – but once Woodward had taken over the management of the international side there was a host of great moments.

There is a sort of symmetry to his playing career in that it started and finished on the ground. He won the first of his 21 caps when he came on as a replacement against Ireland in the Grand Slam season of 1980. Tony Bond suffered a nasty fracture of a leg and Woodward was sent on and remained an integral part of the team for the rest of the season.

His final match was against Wales, which ended in defeat. Prior to that, though, he did face the 1983 All Blacks, when, although he did not add to the four tries he had scored for his

Happy memories of Twickenham... England centre and manager Clive Woodward

Staggering achievement... All Blacks' Invincibles player George Nepia

country, he still played a part in a little bit of English rugby history.

England, under new management, began the reign of coach Dick Greenwood – whose son Will was eventually to play under Woodward – and chairman of selectors Derek Morgan, with the first victory over New Zealand at Twickenham since 1936.

Once again Woodward's memories of the game were rather sketchy. "It was not a great game. I hardly saw the ball all match. They were without their starting front five.

"Don't get me wrong, it was good to win, great to be part of a winning team, but that win was just a one-off and it was not exactly a memorable match. The only good thing about was the win. And there certainly was not a sense that we had taken part in creating a bit of history."

But being inducted to the Twickenham Wall of Fame may well induce that feeling in Woodward. He is joined by one of the all time great players, and New Zealand's finest fullback **George Nepia**.

This outstanding man played in all 30 matches on the 1924-25 tour of Britain and Ireland, making his international debut, aged 19, in the opening test against Ireland. The Tourists did not lose a single match and thus earned themselves the title of 'The Invincibles'.

He won just nine international caps, but made 46 appearances for the All Blacks, 39 of them in succession, a record.

With his staggering talents he could, and should, have won more caps, but in one instance because he was a Maori, he was not allowed on New Zealand's tour of South Africa in 1928 because of the Apartheid regime, and he also missed out on the 1926-27 Maori tour to France, England, Wales and Australia and Sri Lanka because the selectors thought that he was unavailable, in fact at the time he was farming on the remote East Coast.

He switched codes in the 1930s, playing for Streatham and Mitcham and Halifax, but after the Second World War was reinstated as an amateur thanks to an amnesty in 1947.

In 1950 Nepia became the oldest person to play a first class rugby union match when he turned out, aged 45, for the newly-formed Olympians Club at Gisborne. The opponents that day were Poverty Bay, captained by Nepia's eldest son George – another first in New Zealand rugby history. The match, played on September 30th, was won by Olympians 17-11.

Freddie Chapman

England Wing

Born: 1887
(no official record of his precise
date of birth available)
Died: 8.5.1938
Caps: 7
Debut: v Wales 1910
Last app: v Ireland 1914

Cliff Morgan

Wales Outside-half

Born: 7.4.1930
Caps: 29
Debut: v Ireland 1951
Last app: v France 1958

It would be fair to say that **Freddie Chapman** and **Cliff Morgan** could be regarded as the first and last words in Rugby Union, and anyway certainly as far as the World Rugby Museum's Wall of Fame at Twickenham is concerned.

Chapman scored not only the first try at Twickers, but the England right wing also landed the first penalty and the first conversion on the famous old ground.

As for the brilliant, former Wales captain Morgan, he was widely regarded as one of the greatest fly-halves of all time.

He then went on to become a consummate broadcaster, with a wonderful voice, a God-given eye for detail, and a breadth of vocabulary, to describe what he was seeing, which was second to none. He also had another great talent as a broadcaster – knowing just when to speak and how much to say.

The greatest piece of commentary, which sadly did not take place at Twickenham, was the opening of the Barbarians' match against the New Zealand All Blacks at Cardiff Arms Park in 1973. His description of the dazzling, and probably greatest try ever, which was scored by Gareth Edwards, another inductee on to the World Rugby Museum's Wall of Fame, used just 50 words from start to finish. Morgan's commentary though, rather like the try, left everyone speechless with its own brilliance. A brilliance that reflected the touches of genius which eventually carried the ball over the All Blacks' line.

In its own way Chapman's try in the very first match on Billy Williams' Cabbage Patch against Wales in 1910, also had touches of genius to it. And like Edwards' try 63 years later, Chapman's was also scored pretty much from the kick-off.

Adrian Stoop's probing kick sparked a loose scrum. The scrum-half David 'Dai' Gent retrieved the ball and passed to Stoop, thence it went to Barney Solomon, on to John Birkett and finally into the hands of Chapman, who went over on the right for the try, handing off Billy Trew, the Wales captain on the way. A bare 60 seconds had elapsed since Benjamin Gronow had kicked off for Wales.

Although Chapman failed with the conversion, he soon landed a penalty and then added the vital points to Solomon's try shortly before half-time and England managed to hang on for their first win over Wales for 12 years, as well as getting their new headquarters' off to a perfect start.

That was to be Chapman's only try for his country, for whom he played just seven matches. Fast forward 42 years and Morgan trots out on to the hallowed turf for his first international match at Twickenham. He was winning his fourth cap for Wales and confessed: "I remember feeling enormous pride at finding myself playing an international at Twickenham for the first time, [but] I have to admit I also felt a tad nervous as we arrived at the ground."

Morgan, who had made his international debut against Ireland the previous season, was steeped in the lore of a game which transcends all known boundaries.

"I had read avidly about truly immortal [England] figures such as Wavell Wakefield and fly-half, WJA Davies, a brilliant player, who in his book published in 1924 wrote: 'Rugby Football is a mental gymnastics which keeps mind and spirit as fit as wind and limbs. It is a strenuous and manly pursuit which demands devotion. It is a game that sweats the vice out of you.'"

And Morgan admitted that another England player, the aforementioned Adrian Stoop, a fellow Wall of Fame inductee, had also had a huge influence on his approach to rugby.

"My first and lasting memory of Twickenham is of that grand rugby figure, Adrian Stoop, the ever present Harlequin who preached playing with style and adventure. He believed that to play for safety defeats the object of the game for which rugby football was intended. Take risks, as the great wing Obolenski did, was the philosophy of Adrian Stoop. His philosophy influenced my game."

Although one report of the match described the Twickenham surface as "treacherous", as far as Morgan was concerned: "The playing surface at Twickenham was simply perfect for playing running rugby."

He also enjoyed soaking up the atmosphere. "Twickenham seemed to be packed with thousands of loyal, singing Welsh supporters that created an overwhelming sound. The air fairly sizzled with excitement – a fitting prelude for the thrilling match that was to follow." The gates were closed before the kick-off, with an estimated 73,000 in the ground and thousands more locked out.

There is no need to seek out contemporary reports of the action either. Morgan's razor sharp memory can recall it with ease more than half a century later, although he omits mentioning that it was his break and scissors with Ken Jones which earned Wales their opening try.

Morgan provided the commentary: "I remember vividly every move in that game and everyone in that fine England team.

"I was all too aware that I was going to play against England's great fly-half, Nim Hall, and his scrum half, Gordon Rimmer of Waterloo. And what a back-line – Chris Winn and Ted Woodward on the wings. Lewis 'LB' Cannell and Albert Agar in the centre. By the way I had played against Ted Woodward as a schoolboy

"And what a pack England had! Prop forwards, Bob Stirling and hooker Eric Evans of Sale,

Dennis 'Squire' Wilkins and Johnnie Matthews in the second row, and a back row of Alec Lewis of Bath, John Kendall-Carpenter and one of the toughest and truly great flank forwards, Don White of Northampton.

"I remember winning that game as though it was yesterday. A break [by Morgan] from our own 25, then a scissors movement on the half-way line with our Olympic sprinter, Ken Jones, who ran 50 yards to make a glorious try. Then the remarkably talented Lewis Jones, who, despite nursing a torn thigh muscle, came into the threequarter line and made the gap for Ken Jones' second try. For our Captain, John Gwilliam, it was a wonderful victory and for the Welsh supporters an excuse to sing – lifting the spirits of the whole of Wales."

And among that England side was the toughest opponent Morgan ever came across during his distinguished playing career. "Without a doubt my toughest opponent was the great Northampton back-row forward, Don White. Not only did he have the gifts of hardness and tackling and the skill of giving fly-halves, like me, very little room to manoeuvre but he was for me one of the finest rugby brains I came across in my career."

Morgan was to enjoy a further victory at Twickenham, this time as captain of Wales, four years later in 1956. By then he had also wowed the crowds in South Africa as a member, nay, the star, of the 1955 British and Irish Lions, who finished the four-test series against the Springboks all square.

Morgan recalled: "I made a lot of good friends playing matches at Twickenham, many of whom I played with on the 1955 Lions Tour to South Africa, and I obviously remember the thrill of winning in 1956, it was a tough match. It was a great honour to lead Wales on to the ground at Twickenham and it was great that we won the match. I also remember the dinner afterwards – in dinner jackets, as was always the tradition at Twickenham."

Yet, strangely, it was not the 1956 victory which holds the greater place in Morgan's heart. "It was great that we won the 1956 match but, 1952 was THE match. It was the finest hour for me at Twickenham, because we were not expected to win, and Ken Jones showed why he was an Olympic sprinter."

While Morgan remembered the ground fondly, the old Twickenham still had one enduring fault as far as he was concerned. "There was little to dislike about Twickenham, but I wasn't too fond of the wind. The biggest problem was the swirling wind. It seemed to blow from every direction; as we used to say, like the Hurricane Esther. One had no idea in which direction it was blowing – it changed all the time."

True to form though Morgan, like so many other great internationals, recalled with warm pleasure, the baths. "I was immensely impressed with the changing rooms – they were big and warm, with so many showers and *ten* large baths – sheer luxury for those of us who only had very basic facilities back in Cardiff in those days."

And he reiterated his love of the playing surface as well as the proximity of the spectators in the old ground, which created that special, almost intimate atmosphere: "I thought the ground with its beautifully manicured pitch was magic. I loved the closeness of the crowd and there was a great atmosphere which inspired you to try to play winning, attractive rugby."

However, Morgan is no Luddite. He is comfortable with change, with progress and his opinion of the 21st Century Stadium is unstinting. "It is a magnificent stadium and a fine stage for great international matches."

On retiring from playing, Morgan carved himself an outstanding career in broadcasting, finishing up in a lofty position, as he explained: "I took early retirement from the BBC as Head of Outside Broadcasts Group Television which was responsible, at that time, for all the programmes covering sport, national and state events, like royal weddings, the Remembrance Festival, the State Opening of Parliament and so on. I was also the Royal Liaison Officer for the BBC."

Even then there came more. Morgan's eloquent, mellifluous tones were to grace the airwaves for a more than a decade after that. "After I left the BBC I presented a sports programme on BBC Radio 4, Sport on 4, for 12 years every Saturday morning. I also worked for a company called CPMA who owned the broadcasting rights for the first three Rugby World Cups. In addition I was Honorary Chairman of Rugby News."

Chapman started it all for Twickenham 100 years ago and has been followed by an army of talented rugby players ever since. But while Chapman had the first word, Cliff Morgan deserves the final say, after all, for many lovers of the game he was, and still is, the last word in Rugby Union.

Morgan paid tribute to the World Rugby Museum's Wall of Fame, speaking for everyone in the game he said: "I believe it is very important to document the history of rugby at Twickenham and all the people who have contributed to that history.

"Rugby fans from all over the world regard Twickenham as one of the most important grounds for prompting memories of great moments and great players. I really am thrilled and honoured, to be placed on the Wall of Fame alongside so many distinguished rugby players. I feel very humble too."

****

ARGENTINA

Agustin Pichot	152
Hugo Porta	187

AUSTRALIA

David Campese	54
Ken Catchpole	39
Mark Ella	181
Nick Farr-Jones	9
Michael Lynagh	126
Cyril Towers	162
Colin Windon	98

ENGLAND

Rob Andrew	159
Neil Back	21
Bill Beaumont	25
John Birkett	60
Jeff Butterfield	39
Will Carling	187
Freddie Chapman	204
Fran Cotton	28
Ronald Cove-Smith	162
Lawrence Dallaglio	117
W J A Davies	81
Wade Dooley	63
David Duckham	70
Eric Evans	84
Bernard Gadney	9
Jeremy Guscott	103
Richard Hill	93
Bob Hiller	32
Peter Jackson	54
Ron Jacobs	66
Dickie Jeeps	57
Martin Johnson	1
Jason Leonard	123
Cyril Lowe	52
Brian Moore	75
Alexander Obolensky	130

Chris Oti	142
Ronald Poulton	164
Dean Richards	156
Jason Robinson	98
Budge Rogers	35
Hal Sever	170
Richard Sharp	174
Adrian Stoop	12
Rory Underwood	167
Roger Uttley	178
Wavell Wakefield	149
Peter Wheeler	181
Peter Winterbottom	126
Norman Wodehouse	78
Clive Woodward	200

FRANCE

Serge Blanco	70
Didier Codorniou	45
Xavier Dutour	75
Raphael Ibanez	45
Jean Prat	164
Jean-Pierre Rives	178
Philippe Saint-André	149
Philippe Sella	35

IRELAND

Simon Geoghegan	195
Mike Gibson	110
Tom Kiernan	110
Jackie Kyle	25
Willie-John McBride	195
Tony O'Reilly	137
George Stephenson	142
Keith Wood	137

ITALY

Diego Dominguez	60
Massimo Giovanelli	167
Alessandro Troncon	117

NEW ZEALAND

Don Clarke 133
Sean Fitzpatrick 170
John Kirwan 107
Jonah Lomu 93
Colin Meads 130
Graham Mourie 133
George Nepia 200

ROMANIA

Mircea Paraschiv 159

SCOTLAND

Gary Armstrong 16
Gordon Brown 91
Peter Brown 16
Gavin Hastings 84
Andy Irvine 12
Roy Laidlaw 114
Ian Smith 91
Robert Wilson-Shaw 114

SOUTH AFRICA

Gerry Brand 32
Dawie De Villiers 52
Frik Du Preez 66
Hennie Muller 28
Francois Pienaar 78
Chester Williams 42

WALES

Phil Bennett 145
Gerald Davies 87
Gareth Edwards 81
Viv Jenkins 63
Barry John 87
Ken Jones 145
Lewis Jones 191
Cliff Morgan 204
J P R Williams 191